Life Changing Journey

1500 Plus Inspirational Quotes

SERIES II

"Unveiling Wisdom: Inspiring Quotes to Spark Your Life. A Treasury of Inspiration for Cultivating Positivity on Life, Love, Nature, and More."

SHREE SHAMBAV

Life Changing Journey – Series II
1500 Inspirational Quotes
Shree Shambav

Published by Shree Shambav, Tamil Nadu, India

All Rights Reserved
First Edition, 2024
Second Edition 2025
Copyright © 2025, Muniswamy Rajakumar

All rights reserved. No part of this publication may be reproduced, distributed, or transmitted in any form or by any means, including photocopying, recording, or other electronic or mechanical methods, without the author's prior written permission. It is illegal to copy this book, post it to a website, or distribute it by any other means without permission.

The request for permission should be addressed to the author.

ISBN: 978-93-343-2374-0

Email:shreeshambav@gmail.com

Web:www.shambav.org

DEDICATION

"Isavasyam idam sarvam yat kim ca jagatyam jagat, tena tyaktena bhunjitha, ma gridhah kasyasvid dhanam"

To the Almighty,

the Divine Masters,

the family who listens,

and my parents who see –

your presence shapes the pages of my life's journey.

"Isavasyam idam sarvam yat kim ca jagatyam jagat"

Meaning: "God encompasses everything you perceive, see, or touch with your sense organs."

DISCLAIMER

This book, *"Life-Changing Journey - Inspirational Quotes: Series II,"* is a heartfelt compilation of personal reflections and insights born from the author's journey of understanding life and the natural world. Each inspirational quote is a subjective truth—a distillation of experience and thought—meant to serve as a mirror for readers to explore their own perspectives and uncover meaning through the lens of their unique experiences.

The intention behind this book is to share a message imbued with compassion, love, and care. It is designed to inspire readers on their personal journeys and guide them toward discovering the deeper realities of life. This is not a prescriptive manual but an invitation to pause, reflect, and engage with life's profound yet simple truths.

It's important to acknowledge that neither the content nor the sequence of the quotes is intended to cause harm, discomfort, or conflict with the reader's personal beliefs. Should any part of the book feel unsettling or contradictory to one's convictions, it is purely coincidental and never intentional.

The journey through these quotes is one of openness and fluidity, free from rigid interpretations or dogmatic assertions. The content reflects the author's personal perspective and is humbly offered as a source of inspiration and gentle guidance. Readers are invited to engage with the material at their own pace, to reflect deeply, and to adapt the wisdom within to align with their inner truths and life experiences.

Above all, this book aspires to spark joy, nurture connection, and encourage purposeful living. It gently beckons readers to cultivate a life rooted in compassion, integrity, and intentionality while embracing the beauty of each moment with grace and mindfulness. May the words within these pages illuminate your path as you embark on a transformative journey of self-discovery, growth, and renewal. The journey is uniquely yours, and it is an honour for the author to accompany you, even if only in spirit, as you navigate the unfolding of your life.

With this understanding, readers are encouraged to approach the book with an open mind and heart, recognising that its wisdom is offered not as universal truth but as a collection of insights shaped by the author's personal experiences. You are invited to absorb what resonates, reinterpret what feels unfamiliar, and find your own meaning within these words.

Ultimately, the author's deepest wish is that these reflections serve as a beacon of hope, a source of motivation, and a catalyst for positivity as you embark on your life-changing journey. May this book inspire you to walk your path with courage, grace, and an unwavering belief in the beauty of life's unfolding.

Note - If any part of the book, in any sequence, hurts the reader's sentiments, it would be just out of a sheer accident, not intentional

Divine

"In the tender embrace of surrender lies a profound revelation—the raw, unspoken beauty of union. Each ripple of the river becomes a whispered confession, a declaration of belonging to something greater than itself. As the river flows ceaselessly, unveiling its eternal unity with the boundless ocean, so too does the soul, in its sacred act of surrender, unveil its timeless connection to the Divine.

This surrender is not a loss but a metamorphosis of unparalleled grace, where the fragmented self dissolves into the infinite. And in that dissolution, the soul discovers the ineffable depth of its true essence—a profound oneness with the Divine, unbroken and eternal. It is a sacred symphony, an eternal melody that reverberates through the very fabric of existence, calling us back to the home we never truly left."

– Shree Shambav

SHREE SHAMBAV

EPIGRAM

"A single whisper of truth can echo through eternity—
guiding the lost, healing the broken,
and awakening the soul to the light it always carried within."

– Shree Shambav

Life Changing Journey

1500 Plus Inspirational Quotes

Shree Shambav

Shree Shambav is a 40x best-selling author renowned for his transformative works in personal development and spiritual growth.

Dear Cherished Readers

Dear Cherished Readers,

As I embark on this new literary voyage, my heart swells with profound gratitude and an overwhelming sense of connection. With deep emotion, I extend my heartfelt appreciation to each of you who has joined me on this journey.

With sincere warmth, I invite you to revisit the steps we have taken together through the pages of my earlier works. Our odyssey began with "Journey of Soul - Karma," a book that marked my first foray into the world of words and a testament to the raw passion that ignited my writing adventure.

The subsequent chapters of our shared narrative unfolded through the enchanting tapestry of the "Twenty + One" series. Each page turned was a brushstroke on the canvas of our imaginations, painting vivid stories that I hoped would resonate deeply within your hearts.

And how can I forget the transformative journey we embarked on with the "Life Changing Journey - Inspirational Quotes Series." Day by day, quote by quote, we delved into reflections that uplifted, inspired, and sought to bring a glimpse of light to our souls.

The release of "Death - Light of Life and the Shadow of Death" promises to shed new light on the timeless mystery of death.

The **Optimum Python Series** is a comprehensive guide designed to empower readers at every stage of their programming journey. It begins with *Series I: Ultimate Guide for Beginners*, which lays a strong foundation in Python, making it accessible and engaging for newcomers. *Series II: Exploring Data Structures and Algorithms* takes the next step, offering a deep dive into core computer science principles that enhance problem-solving skills and coding efficiency. Building on this, *Series III: Python Power for Data Science* introduces powerful libraries such as NumPy, Pandas, Matplotlib, and Scikit-learn, guiding readers through data manipulation, visualisation, and foundational machine learning techniques. Finally, *Series IV: Unleashing the Potential of Data Science with Machine Learning Techniques* explores advanced machine learning models and real-world applications, enabling readers to harness the full potential of data-driven insights. Whether you're just starting out or looking to master sophisticated tools and strategies, this series is your roadmap to Python proficiency and beyond.

Shree Shambav expands his artistic repertoire with *"Whispers of Eternity: 150 Plus - A Symphony of Soulful Verses,"* a heartfelt exploration of the human experience. Alongside this, his *"Whispers of the Soul: A Journey Through Haiku"* distils profound insights into poignant verses. Together, these works showcase his versatility and mastery of soulful expression, inviting readers on a journey of self-discovery. Through his poetry, he weaves a rich tapestry of emotion that resonates deeply with the heart.

Shree Shambav's latest works—*Learn to Love Yourself: A Journey of Discovering Inner Beauty and Strength Through 10 Transformative Rules, The Power of Letting Go: Embrace Freedom and Happiness, A Journey of Lasting Peace*—are true treasures of self-discovery, *The Entitlement Trap: Get Over It, Get On, Whispers of a Dying Soul: Unspoken Regrets and Unlived Dreams, Whispers of Silence - Unlocking Inner Power through Stillness, The Power of Words: Transforming Speech, Transforming Lives, The Art of Intentional Living: Minimalism for a Life of Purpose, Awakening the Infinite: The Power of Consciousness in Transforming Life, Beyond the Veil: A Journey Through Life After Death series, Bonds Beyond Blood - Where love builds bridges, and bonds defy blood., A Journey into Spiritual Maturity - 12 Golden Rules for Inner Transformation, The Seeker's Gold: Unlocking Life's Greatest Treasure and The Power of Manifestation - Unlocking The Path From Thought To Reality.*

In addition to these works, Shree Shambav has recently ventured into astrology with the release of Astrology Unveiled – Foundations of Ancient Wisdom Series I to VIII, expanding into the realm of metaphysics. These books explore the foundational principles of Vedic astrology, offering readers a rich and practical understanding of this ancient wisdom.

Your unwavering support, enthusiasm to immerse yourself in my writings, and readiness to embark on these journeys with me have been my greatest sources of inspiration. Your input has been a beacon guiding me through the creation process, moulding these stories into containers of passion, emotion, knowledge, and resonance.

As I unveil this new narrative before you, know that your presence, insights, and shared moments have been my companions. The path we have walked together is etched in the annals of my creative evolution, and it's an honour beyond words to have you by my side once more.

Here's to the readers who have illuminated my path with their presence, who have embraced my stories with open hearts, and who have woven themselves into the very fabric of my literary world. Our journey has been a symbiotic dance of writer and reader, a harmony of souls brought together by the magic of storytelling.

With a heart brimming with appreciation and eyes glistening with anticipation, I extend my deepest gratitude for your unwavering support. Thank you for the memories, the shared emotions, and the countless hours spent in the worlds we've crafted together. As we step into this new adventure, let's continue to explore, feel, and discover the boundless horizons that words can unveil.

Warmly,

Shree Shambav

LIFE CHANGING JOURNEY

Suggested Reads

FROM BEST-SELLING AUTHOR

Endorsements

"*Life Changing Journey – Inspirational Quotes Series II* is a luminous guide for the soul—gentle in its tone yet profound in its impact. Shree Shambav has masterfully curated a treasury of timeless truths, each quote a spark of wisdom capable of lighting the darkest moments of our lives. This collection is more than inspirational—it is transformational.

With themes ranging from inner strength and resilience to love, gratitude, and divine connection, the book offers solace to the weary, courage to the dreamer, and peace to the seeker. Each page feels like a quiet conversation with the soul, reminding us that we are not alone in our struggles or our triumphs. Whether you are navigating change, searching for meaning, or simply yearning for hope, this book will meet you where you are and gently guide you forward.

Shree Shambav's words don't just inspire—they awaken. *Life Changing Journey* is a companion for anyone seeking a more intentional, soulful, and empowered way of living. I wholeheartedly recommend this beautiful work to all who believe in the healing and guiding power of words."

- UMA Devi (Entrepreneur)

About the Author

Shree Shambav is an internationally acclaimed, best-selling author, inspirational speaker, artist, philanthropist, life coach, and entrepreneur. A world record holder, his deep passion for music led him to create soul-stirring albums, drawing inspiration from his celebrated poetry collection, Whispers of Eternity. His profound insights have sparked deep personal transformations, guiding countless individuals toward self-discovery, purposeful living, and authenticity.

With an extraordinary ability to unlock human potential, Shree empowers individuals to break through limitations and embrace their highest selves. His writings, lectures, and compassionate guidance continue to uplift lives, fostering resilience, mindfulness, and personal growth.

Shree Shambav is a 40x best-selling author celebrated for his profound contributions to personal development and spiritual growth.

Shree Shambav's literary journey took flight with the celebrated Journey of Soul - Karma, where he delved into the depths of human experience to unveil profound insights. Garnering recognition through multiple literature awards, his repertoire includes esteemed works, such as the Twenty + One Series and the enlightening Life Changing Journey series.

As a distinguished alumnus of the Indian Institute of Management and the National Institute of Technology, Shree Shambav brings a wealth of corporate acumen from his tenure in multinational corporations. His most recent publications, including Unveiling the Enigma, Death - Light of Life and the Shadow of Death and Optimum - Python Series I, Series II, Series III and Series IV, demonstrate his mastery of both the literary and technical spheres.

Shree Shambav expands his artistic repertoire with "*Whispers of Eternity: 150 Plus - A Symphony of Soulful Verses*," a heartfelt exploration of the human experience. Alongside this, his "*Whispers of the Soul: A Journey Through Haiku*" distils profound insights into poignant verses. Together, these works showcase his versatility and mastery of soulful expression, inviting readers on a journey of self-discovery. Through his poetry, he weaves a rich tapestry of emotion that resonates deeply with the heart.

Shree Shambav's latest works—*Learn to Love Yourself: A Journey of Discovering Inner Beauty and Strength Through 10 Transformative Rules, The Power of Letting Go: Embrace Freedom and Happiness, A*

LIFE CHANGING JOURNEY

Journey of Lasting Peace—are true treasures of self-discovery, The Entitlement Trap: Get Over It, Get On, Whispers of a Dying Soul: Unspoken Regrets and Unlived Dreams, Whispers of Silence - Unlocking Inner Power through Stillness, The Power of Words: Transforming Speech, Transforming Lives, The Art of Intentional Living: Minimalism for a Life of Purpose, Awakening the Infinite: The Power of Consciousness in Transforming Life, Beyond the Veil: A Journey Through Life After Death series, Bonds Beyond Blood - Where love builds bridges, and bonds defy blood., A Journey into Spiritual Maturity - 12 Golden Rules for Inner Transformation, The Seeker's Gold: Unlocking Life's Greatest Treasure and The Power of Manifestation - Unlocking The Path From Thought To Reality.

In addition to these works, Shree Shambav has recently ventured into astrology with the release of Astrology Unveiled – Foundations of Ancient Wisdom Series I to VIII, expanding into the realm of metaphysics. These books explore the foundational principles of Vedic astrology, offering readers a rich and practical understanding of this ancient wisdom.

Shree Shambav established the Ayur Rakshita Foundation, which is dedicated to promoting boundless growth, universal fraternity, and environmental protection. The charity helps diverse communities while working for societal progress.

To learn more about Shree Shambav and his works, visit his website at www.shambav.org. For information about the Ayur Rakshita Foundation and its initiatives, visit www.shambav-ayurrakshita.org.

Let's Follow him on Social Media: **@shreeshambav**

Main: https://linktr.ee/shreeshambav

SHREE SHAMBAV

Website: https://www.shambav.org/

LinkedIn: https://www.linkedin.com/in/shreeshambav/

Blog: https://blog.shambav.org/

Instagram: https://www.instagram.com/shreeshambav/

YouTube: https://www.youtube.com/@shreeshambav

Amazon: https://www.amazon.com/author/shreeshambav

Goodreads: https://www.goodreads.com/author/show/22367436.Shree_Shambav

PREFACE

Life is a symphony, and each moment plays its own note in the grand orchestration of existence. Within this ever-evolving melody, words hold a sacred and timeless power—they awaken dormant truths, soothe invisible wounds, and ignite the spirit with renewed hope. *Life Changing Journey – Inspirational Quotes Series* by Shree Shambav is far more than a collection of phrases; it is a soulful companion, a quiet guide, and a radiant beacon for those traversing the intricate and often uncertain pathways of life.

This book was conceived in the stillness where true inspiration breathes—in those sacred pauses when the noise of the world recedes, and the voice of the soul begins to rise. Each quote is a drop of distilled wisdom, a mirror reflecting universal truths through the lens of simplicity and depth. These words echo the shared heartbeat of human experience, inviting the reader into a contemplative space where healing, clarity, and transformation quietly unfold.

Structured with intention and grace, each chapter explores a unique dimension of the human spirit. They illuminate the courage it takes to embrace change, the resilience needed to pursue dreams, and the wisdom found in the face of adversity. They explore the tenderness of love, the beauty of authentic self-acceptance, and the quiet power that lies dormant within us all. These pages whisper of joy rooted in simplicity, gratitude awakened by mindfulness, and the sacred interconnectedness we share with nature, the cosmos, and one another.

This book is a living tapestry of timeless insights—threads of light woven to transcend circumstance and awaken the soul. It invites you to pause, reflect, and reconnect with the deeper wisdom that resides within. Whether you are weathering personal storms, seeking the spark to chase your aspirations, or longing for inner stillness and peace, the quotes within offer not just inspiration but companionship for the road ahead. A trusted confidant through life's journey, this collection invites you to discover the power of presence, purpose, and the quiet miracles waiting in every moment.

Life Changing Journey – Inspirational Quotes Series I beautifully explores the many dimensions of human experience. Through themes like Karma, Divinity, True Love, and Cosmic Principles, it offers deep reflections on life, purpose, and wisdom. Each chapter invites the reader to pause, reflect, and grow from within.

In Series II, "Life Changing Journey – Inspirational Quotes Series II", gracefully weaves together a rich tapestry of themes that reflect the many layers of the human experience. This collection explores the journey of Discovering Self and nurturing Dreams and Aspirations, while embracing life's inevitable transitions through Embracing Change and Embracing Imperfections. It offers strength through Finding Inner Strength, and serenity through Gratitude and Mindfulness. The series uplifts with Inspiration and Motivation, imparts resilience through Lessons from

Adversity, and celebrates the depth of Love and Relationships. It honours the harmony found in Nature's Symphony and encourages the pursuit of purpose in Pursuing Your Dreams. With reflections on Serenity and Balance, Shades of Existence, and Success and Achievement, it invites readers to find meaning in The Beauty of Simplicity and The Power of Kindness. The journey culminates in soulful reflections such as Whispers of the Divine and timeless Wisdom from the Ages, offering profound insight and guidance for every step of life's path."

Series III, themes like *"Embracing Change," "Discovering Self," "Dreams and Aspirations," "Embracing Imperfections," "Finding Inner Strength,"* and *"Gratitude and Mindfulness"* invite you to reflect on identity, purpose, and the pursuit of your passions.

Series IV delves deeper into *"Inspiration and Motivation," "Lessons from Adversity," "Love and Relationships," "Nature's Symphony," "Pursuing Your Dreams,"* and *"Serenity and Balance"*— nurturing connections, fostering resilience, and celebrating life's harmony.

Series V culminates in the profound, with themes like *"Shades of Existence," "Success and Achievement," "The Beauty of Simplicity," "The Power of Kindness,"* and *"Wisdom from the Ages."* These chapters remind us to cherish the beauty in life's simplest moments and draw strength from timeless truths.

Series VI culminates in a journey of inner stillness and soulful reflection, exploring themes such as *"Embracing Change," "Love and Relationships," "Serenity and Balance," "Shades of Existence,"* and *"Whispers of the Divine."* Each chapter gently invites us to slow down, to find meaning in silence, and to recognise the sacred in everyday life. They are reminders that life's simplest moments often carry the most profound truths and that true strength arises when we listen deeply—to others, to nature, and to our hearts.

Series VII deepens this introspection, guiding us through themes like *"Discovering the Self," "Finding Inner Strength," "Lessons from Adversity," "The Power of Kindness,"* and *"Wisdom from the Ages."*

Series VIII invites readers on a deeper path of introspection, embracing themes like change, imperfections, and inner strength.

Rooted in mindfulness, gratitude, and inspiration, it nurtures quiet resilience and clarity.

Through nature's rhythms and life's simple truths, it gently reminds us that lasting transformation begins within.

These chapters serve as lanterns on the path of growth—illuminating how hardship refines us, how kindness transforms, and how the wisdom of those who walked before us still echoes with relevance today. They remind us that every challenge holds a lesson, and every moment offers a choice to awaken.

Shree Shambav's words transcend the mundane, touching the sacred essence of life. They serve as gentle reminders of our shared humanity, encouraging us to embrace imperfections and live authentically. Each quote is a spark—a catalyst for growth and self-discovery, illuminating the path through life's trials and triumphs.

LIFE CHANGING JOURNEY

As you turn these pages, may you find not just words but a profound connection to your inner self and the world around you. Let this collection be a sanctuary of wisdom, a reservoir of courage, and a wellspring of inspiration, empowering you to embrace life with an open heart and an awakened soul.

Welcome to the *"Life Changing Journey - Inspirational Quotes Series."* May this book inspire you to live boldly, love deeply, and discover the boundless joy within your own journey.

Let the journey unfold.

With gratitude and encouragement,

Shree Shambav

INTRODUCTION

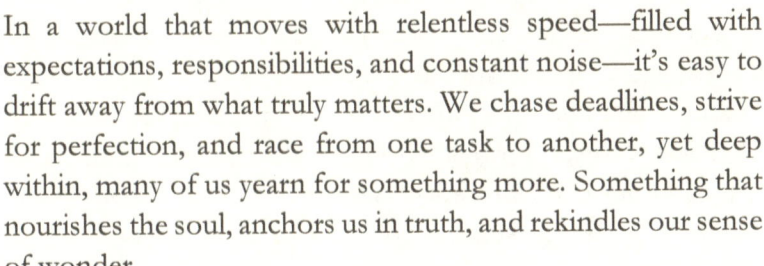

In a world that moves with relentless speed—filled with expectations, responsibilities, and constant noise—it's easy to drift away from what truly matters. We chase deadlines, strive for perfection, and race from one task to another, yet deep within, many of us yearn for something more. Something that nourishes the soul, anchors us in truth, and rekindles our sense of wonder.

That quiet yearning—the whisper beneath the rush—is the seed from which the *Life Changing Journey – Inspirational Quotes Series* was born. This book is not merely a collection of quotes; it is an invitation. A gentle call to pause, to reflect, and to remember the deeper wisdom that surrounds us and lives within us.

Words, when offered with sincerity and soul, have the power to change the course of a day—or a life. A single phrase, encountered at the right moment, can offer clarity in chaos, light in darkness, or courage in fear. This collection was curated with that transformative potential in mind. Each quote is a distillation of timeless truths, crafted to awaken the strength, hope, and resilience that already dwell within you.

This second volume of the series—*Life Changing Journey – Inspirational Quotes Series II*—unfolds as a soul-guided journey across the landscapes of the human spirit. It gently walks you through themes such as *Discovering*

Self and *Nurturing Dreams and Aspirations*, inviting you to embrace *Change* and *Imperfection* with grace. It helps uncover your *Inner Strength*, deepen your experience of *Gratitude and Mindfulness*, and rekindle *Inspiration and Motivation* in every chapter.

You'll find courage in stories of *Adversity*, joy in *Love and Relationships*, and harmony through *Nature's Symphony*. You'll be encouraged to *Pursue Your Dreams*, cultivate *Serenity and Balance*, and appreciate the nuanced *Shades of Existence*. Chapters on *Success and Achievement*, *The Beauty of Simplicity*, and *The Power of Kindness* provide both insight and grounding. And as the journey deepens, reflections on *Whispers of the Divine* and *Wisdom from the Ages* serve as soulful reminders of your eternal connection to something greater.

These are not just themes—they are stepping stones for transformation. Each one invites you to see life not merely as a series of events but as a sacred unfolding of who you truly are. They gently guide you to find beauty in imperfection, strength in stillness, and clarity in silence.

This book is not meant to be consumed in one sitting. It is meant to be lived with. Revisited. Rediscovered. Like a trusted friend, it will meet you where you are—whether you are standing at a crossroads, moving through a challenge, or celebrating a quiet victory. In moments of doubt, may these words bring assurance. In times of transition, may they offer direction. And in moments of joy, may they deepen your gratitude.

In an age when the world constantly pulls us outward, this book gently invites you inward—to reconnect with your inner compass, to realign with your truth, and to remember that the answers you seek often rise from stillness.

As you turn its pages, I hope you find more than inspiration. I hope you find connection. With yourself. With others. And with the wonder that lives quietly in each moment. May these quotes serve not only as reflections of truth, but as a light to illuminate your unique path.

This is your journey. Your sacred unfolding. May these words give you the courage to live it fully, authentically, and with grace.

With love and gratitude,

Shree Shambav

PROLOGUE

The Soul's Silent Compass

There are moments in life when the world grows quiet—not because there is no sound, but because the noise no longer matters. In those rare spaces of stillness, we begin to hear something deeper. Not from the outside, but from within. A whisper. A calling. A reminder.

That we are more than what we chase.

More than what we fear.

More than what the world asks us to be.

In the quiet corridors of the heart, a different kind of wisdom lives—one not shaped by circumstances, but by essence. It is here, in this sacred inward gaze, that true transformation begins.

This book is born from such silence.

Life Changing Journey – Inspirational Quotes Series II is not merely a compilation of uplifting words; it is a reflection of the soul's timeless dialogue with life. These quotes are echoes—fragments of truth that have travelled through the storms of adversity, the warmth of love, the fire of ambition, and the serenity of acceptance.

Each quote is a spark—a reminder of the light within you. They do not offer instructions or rigid answers. Instead, they invite inquiry, introspection, and awakening. They meet you wherever you are—whether you're standing on the threshold of change, navigating the shadows of doubt, or basking in the quiet joy of presence.

This second volume continues a journey that began with a simple question:

What truly changes a life?

Not merely success, or accolades, or the fulfilment of dreams. But awareness. Courage. Love. Gratitude. Resilience. The ability to return to oneself, again and again, with gentleness and truth.

As you walk through these pages, you may find verses that stir memories, bring comfort, or ignite a forgotten fire within. Some may feel like old friends; others like sacred mirrors. Each quote has been selected not for its brilliance alone, but for its ability to touch the ineffable—those truths we know not by thought, but by heart.

Let this book be your companion—not just in clarity, but in confusion. Not only in triumph, but in your most tender unravelling. It is in those vulnerable places where real wisdom takes root.

Life is not a straight road. It is a dance. A surrender. A rising and a falling.

But through it all, there are moments—precious and few—where we pause long enough to remember:

We are not alone.

We are not broken.

We are becoming.

May these words walk beside you as a gentle guide. May they remind you of your inner radiance. And may they illuminate the quiet path that leads back home—to your truth, your wholeness, your soul.

Welcome to the journey.— *Shree Shambav*

CONTENTS

DEDICATION iii
DISCLAIMER v
Divine vii
EPIGRAM ix
Dear Cherished Readers xiii
Suggested Reads xvii
Endorsements xix
About the Author xxi
PREFACE xxv
INTRODUCTION xxxi
PROLOGUE xxxv
Embracing Change 1
   Navigating Life's Transformations 1
Pursue your dreams 21
   Overcoming Obstacles 21
Discovering Self 45
   Reflections on Identity and Purpose 45
Love and Relationships 75
   Nurturing Connections 75
Finding Inner Strength 105
   Empowering the Mind and Spirit 105
Embracing Imperfections 131
   Embracing Self-Acceptance 131

Gratitude and Mindfulness 155
   Finding Joy in the Present 155
Inspiration and Motivation 179
   Fuelling the Soul 179
Dreams and Aspirations 205
   Dreams and Aspirations 205
Lessons from Adversity 227
   Turning Challenges into Growth 227
The Power of Kindness 253
   Spreading Compassion and Love 253
Wisdom from the Ages 281
   Timeless Insights for Life 281
Serenity and Balance 311
   Cultivating Inner Peace 311
Success and Achievement 335
   Unleashing Your Potential 335
The Beauty of Simplicity 359
   Embracing Life's Little Pleasures 359
Nature Symphony 387
   Odes to the Earth 387
Whispers of the Divine 419
   Cosmic connection 419
Shades of Existence 451
   Light of Life 451

Blossoming Life 485
  A Priceless Dance 485
Life Coach and Philanthropist 489
TESTIMONIALS 491
ACKNOWLEDGEMENTS 499

Embracing Change
Navigating Life's Transformations

"In the ebb and flow of life's transformations, we discover the strength to weather storms and the grace to embrace new horizons."

- *Shree Shambav*

Appreciating Life's Gifts

"Learn to appreciate the gifts that life bestows on you because they serve as the foundation for your unique journey."

Architect of Your Life

"You are the architect of your own life. Each day is a new canvas and every choice you make is a stroke of the brush. Create your masterpiece one day at a time, and never be afraid to try new things or take chances. Your life is your own, and it is up to you to make it a work of art."

Authenticity of Unspoken Thoughts

"We find the true canvas of another's reality in the unspoken. The silent symphony of their unspoken thoughts paints a more profound portrait than words could ever do."

Bravery in Risk-Taking

"While going down in flames is painful, it demonstrates your bravery and willingness to take risks."

Burning Brighter After Flames

"When everything seems to be lost and you're on the verge of burning out, remember that sometimes you have to go down in flames to light the way for a brighter future."

Carrying Joy

"Carrying joy in your heart allows you to find beauty in the most unexpected places, turning ordinary moments into cherished memories."

Caution in Desires

"The hues of attachment are painted on the canvas of human emotions, giving rise to desires that bloom like flowers. Yet, be wary, for beneath these cravings lie dormant seeds of rage, waiting for the right moment to sprout."

Celebrating Self

"Celebrate yourself and honour the fact that you are your best thing, a unique and irreplaceable expression of life."

Cherishing Impermanence

"Life's transience is a poignant reminder that every moment is a treasure, every step a fleeting journey, and every embrace a temporary solace. We find the beauty of cherishing what we have in its impermanence, for it is with time that we discover the true value of each heartbeat."

Cultivating Joy

"Joy is not a destination; it is a state of mind that we cultivate through gratitude, mindfulness, and keeping an open heart to the wonders of life."

Daring Pursuit of Dreams

"Going down in flames is not a sign of failure, but that you dared to push boundaries and pursue your dreams with unwavering passion."

Defining Moments

"What defines us is not the circumstances we face, but how we respond to them. We are defined by our character, our resilience, and our ability to rise above adversity. No matter what life throws our way, we have the power to choose how we will respond and the strength to overcome any challenge."

Discovering Inner Strength

"The journey through wild, uncharted waters tests our mettle, but it's in these uncharted depths that we uncover our true strength and resilience."

Discovering Truth in Darkness

"When things are in their darkest, we discover our deepest truths and create a stronger version of ourselves."

Embrace Authenticity

"Hold on to your authenticity, for it is what makes you unique and allows you to shine your light in the world."

Embracing Adversity

"Faced with adversity, embrace the flames that threaten to consume you, for it is only in the fire that you will find the strength to reinvent yourself."

Embracing Life's Challenges

"It's not the circumstances of our lives that define us, but how we choose to respond to them. Our character and strength are forged in the challenges we face and the decisions we make. Embrace life's difficulties as opportunities for growth and never give up on what truly matters to you."

Embracing Mistakes

"Embrace mistakes as essential lessons on life's journey; they are the stepping stones to growth and wisdom."

Embracing Moments of Stillness

"In the embrace of moments of stillness, we discover that silence is not an absence, but a presence—an invitation to listen to our soul's whispers and the secrets of the universe."

Embracing Mysteries

"Embrace the mysteries that emerge in the wake of perplexing revelations; they hold the keys to your growth."

Embracing Self-Acceptance

"Embrace your flaws, your strengths, and every aspect of your being, because it is only through self-acceptance that you can truly become your best self."

Embracing Self-Worth

"Embrace the truth that you are your best thing, for within you lie immeasurable worth and potential."

Embracing Stillness

"Embracing moments of stillness is akin to sipping from the cup of eternity, where time stands still, and we become one with the universe. It is in these pauses that we find the deepest truths and the greatest clarity."

Endurance of Pain

"The endurance of pain is not the end, but the beginning of a journey into the uncharted territories of our own resilience and profound existence."

Endurance of Truth

"The lifespan of a lie may be fleeting, lasting only a few hours, but the endurance of truth stretches across the expanse of eternity."

Every Step Counts

"The journey of a thousand miles starts with a single step. Don't wait for the perfect moment, the perfect conditions, or the perfect plan. Start where you are, with what you have, and take the first step towards your dreams. Every step counts, no matter how small."

Finding Strength in Challenges

"Sometimes, life's gifts come wrapped in challenges, but within those challenges lies the opportunity to find strength and resilience."

Giving Your All

"Give it your all, because greatness awaits those who rise to the occasion with unwavering determination."

Going the Extra Mile

"Go the extra mile. The difference between average and exceptional is just a little extra effort. Put in the work and go above and beyond what is expected of you, and you will see the rewards of your labours. Don't settle for mediocrity; strive for excellence and leave a lasting impact."

Gratitude as a Bridge

"When appreciation seems distant, let gratitude be the bridge that connects hearts."

Growth in Darkness

"Within the depths of darkness lies the potential for profound growth and transformation, because it is in the shadows that we discover our true essence."

Guidance of Values

"Hold fast to your values, for they are the compass that guides your actions and shapes your character."

Holding onto Dreams

"Hold on to your dreams, because they are the blueprints for your future and the source of inspiration that fuels your journey."

Holding onto Faith

"Hold on to your faith, for it is the anchor that keeps you steady amidst the uncertainties of life and gives you the courage to face challenges."

Holding onto Gratitude

"Hold on to gratitude, for it reminds you of the blessings in your life and helps you cultivate a positive perspective."

Holding onto Hope

"Hold onto hope, because it is the fuel that ignites dreams and propels us forward in the face of adversity."

Holding onto Inner Strength

"Hold onto your inner strength, because it is the foundation upon which you can weather any storm and emerge stronger than before."

Holding onto Love

"Hold onto love, because it is the greatest gift we can give and receive, and it has the power to heal and transform lives."

Holding onto Passions

"Hold on to your passions, for they are the sparks that ignite your soul and give purpose to your existence."

Inner Light in Darkness

"On the canvas of our darkest moments, our inner light paints its most vivid colours."

Internal Reflection

"Everything you gaze upon, be it the things you cherish or those you scorn, exists within you to varying degrees."

Joy's Contagious Nature

"When you have joy in your heart, it becomes contagious, spreading its light to everyone you meet."

Learning from Mistakes

"Mistakes serve as a reminder that life's canvas is not perfect, but it's the imperfections that make it a masterpiece worth cherishing."

Life as a Masterpiece

"Your life is your masterpiece, and you are the artist. Every experience, every decision, every moment is an opportunity to create something beautiful and meaningful. So, take control of the brush, and paint the picture you want for your life. Make it a masterpiece that reflects your passions, your values, and your dreams."

Life's Unexpected Gifts

"Life's gifts may appear in unexpected forms but always contain priceless lessons and life-changing experiences."

Making the Most of Life

"Do what you can with what you have, where you are. Life is a journey, and sometimes it can be overwhelming, but it's important to remember that you have the power to make a difference in your own life and the lives of those around you. Use what you have, work with what you've got, and always strive to do your best."

Mindset and Joy

"Embrace the truth that joy does not happen to us; it reflects our mindset and choices."

Moving Past Shadows

"Let the shadows fall behind you. As you move forward and pursue your dreams, don't let your fears and doubts hold you back. Keep your eyes fixed on your goals and let your confidence and determination guide you. The shadows may linger for a time, but with persistence and perseverance, they will eventually fade into the distance."

Natural Positivity

"When joy becomes a natural part of who you are, positivity and abundance will easily flow into your life."

Passion and Greatness

"Wholehearted passion gives birth to greatness - half-heartedness breeds mediocrity."

Perception of Beauty

"An optimist is enthralled by the beauty of a lotus flower that has grown from filth and is clean and pure, whereas a pessimist is concerned about the filth it grew from and cannot recognise the beauty that has emerged."

Readiness for Transformation

"It's never too late to introspect and ask, 'Am I prepared for a transformative journey? Can I evolve from within?'"

Recognising Self-Worth

"You can define your worth and chart your course. Never lose sight of the fact that you are your best asset."

Rediscovering Stillness

"Amidst the chaos of life's relentless rhythm, stillness is the sanctuary where we rediscover our inner compass, aligning ourselves with the essence of our being and the cadence of existence."

Refreshment in Nature

"Getting your hands in the soil can be relaxing. Because of the fresh air and new ideas, you'll feel more energised."

Revitalisation and Rebirth

"At every heartbeat and with every new breath, one should experience revitalisation and rebirth."

Rise Beyond the Shell

"You are not your limitations. You are the space between your fear and your becoming—the crack where light dares to enter and transform."

Shaping by Life's Offerings

"Life's offerings may not always align with your expectations, but they are tailor-made to shape you into the person you were meant to be."

Solitude for Self-Reflection

"Solitude is the choice to be alone for self-reflection and happiness."

Starting the Journey

"It doesn't matter where you start; what's important is that you start. Every journey begins with a single step, so take that step today and start pursuing your dreams. No matter where you are in life, it's never too late to begin creating the future you want."

Stone's Wisdom

"A mountain does not rush to grow, nor a forest race to rise—yet they endure, not through force, but by being wholly themselves. So too, the soul must learn the art of grounded becoming."

Transformation in Adversity

"Don't be afraid to go down in flames, because it is often in the ashes that you find the seeds of transformation and growth."

Understanding Oneself

"In the symphony of life, comprehending others is an intellectual note, but finding the melody within oneself is the sublime wisdom that resonates with the soul."

Understanding Others

"To understand another, delve into the unspoken realms, for there, in the silence, you'll find the authentic tapestry of their existence."

Wisdom of Self-Discovery

"Discerning others is a testament to intelligence, but unravelling the intricacies of oneself is the embodiment of true wisdom."

Pursue your dreams
Overcoming Obstacles

"Obstacles are not roadblocks, but invitations to grow. They put us to the test, showing us that the greatest victories often come from the most difficult conflicts."

- Shree Shambav

Action Over Fear

"Fear is just an emotion. It is not true. The only true thing is the action you take, regardless."

Allure of Adversity

"Life's allure lies in the challenges we face, for it is adversity that fosters resilience, embraces growth, and ultimately reveals the true essence of our being."

Art of Understanding

"To fathom the depths of others is an art of the mind, yet to navigate the labyrinth within is the profound journey of the wise heart."

Beauty in Suffering

"The threads of suffering weave the most beautiful stories in the tapestry of life. Scars mar the canvas, but they also add depth, beauty, and the ability to inspire."

Belief in Yourself

"Believe in yourself and your abilities, and the universe will work with you to bring your dreams to fruition."

Beyond Giving Up

"Quitters never see the extraordinary possibilities that lie just beyond the point of giving up."

Brushstrokes of Perfection

"In the intricate design of life, every moment, be it minuscule or monumental, is a brushstroke of perfection on the canvas of our existence, scripted by a divine plan unfolding through time."

Calm in the Storm

"In the storm of life, be the calm centre that radiates strength and serenity, even under the most tremendous pressure."

Changing the World

"By being true to yourself and defending what you believe in, you can change the world."

Choice of Hard Work

"While intelligence is a gift, hard work is a choice that can transform mediocrity into excellence."

Choices and Fate

"Our choices weave the threads of happiness and sorrow long before they cover the loom of our lives, serving as a constant reminder that the choices we make determine our fate."

Confronting Pain

"Running from pain is like evading shadows; we must confront it to see the brilliance of the light that awaits on the other side."

Cosmic Symphony

"In poetic musings on the universe, we catch a glimpse of the cosmic symphony, where stars are the notes and galaxies are the verses, and in every celestial stanza, we find the melody of existence."

Courageous Exploration

"Life is a courageous exploration of who you are capable of becoming, not a quest to find yourself."

Destined Encore

"Success shall be your destined encore if you embrace the constancy of your goals and unwavering effort."

Dreams Fuel Passion

"Dreams fuel your passion, ignite your determination, and empower you to overcome obstacles on your path to greatness."

LIFE CHANGING JOURNEY

Dreams and Achievements

"Dreams are the seeds of extraordinary achievements; nurture them with belief and action, and watch them flourish."

Embrace Change

"In the face of change, do not be afraid to spread your wings and let the winds guide you to new horizons."

Embrace the Depths

"In our efforts to avoid pain, we inadvertently avoid the depths of our true selves. Embrace the pain because it leads to a deeper understanding of who you are beyond the shadows of suffering."

Embrace the Motion

"The beauty of a journey lies in its never-ending motion. Continue to move forward while accepting the constantly shifting path in front of you."

Embracing Change

"Butterflies are a gentle reminder to welcome change with open minds and hearts, because only through transformation can we truly find our wings."

Embracing Emptiness

"Let go of the past, discard your preconceptions, and become an empty page. You can create your future in emptiness."

Embracing Lessons

"We must learn to let go of the things in life that hold us back and embrace the lessons that will propel us forward."

Embracing Life's Messiness

"The mud-lusciousness of spring is a reminder to embrace life's messiness and to find beauty in unexpected places."

Embracing the Extraordinary

"To embrace the extraordinary within is to transcend the ordinary, and this is where the true magic of life unfolds."

Essence of Intelligence and Hard Work

"Intelligence without hard work is like a ship without a captain; it may have potential, but it won't reach its destination."

Firm Resilience

"We must stand firm in the face of the ferocious wind, like the roots of a tree that anchor us to the earth."

Focus Forward

"Don't get caught up in the past; instead, focus on the path ahead and the opportunities that await."

Forward with Purpose

"In your journey, do not linger in the past; instead, keep moving forward with purpose and determination."

Gateway to Self-Discovery

"In the pursuit of escape, we often forget that within the pain lies the gateway to discovering the depth of our true selves."

Hope in Darkness

"Fairy tales are not just for children; they also teach adults that there is always hope, even in the darkest of times."

Inner Brilliance

"Like a diamond forged under immense pressure, your inner focus and unwavering calm in the face of adversity will reveal your true brilliance."

Inspiration at the Top

"On top of the world, we find inspiration and motivation, knowing that if we can conquer mountains, we can conquer anything else that comes our way."

Internal Cultivation

"Stop looking for yourself in the external world and start cultivating the qualities, values, and passions that make you uniquely you."

Inward Reflection

"Rather than looking outside for answers, look within and recognise that life is a beautiful opportunity to create, evolve, and transform."

Journey of Self-Discovery

"Life is a journey of self-discovery, and the lessons we learn along the way help us become the best versions of ourselves."

Leap of Faith

"When an opportunity presents itself, don't let fear hold you back. Take a deep breath, gather your strength, and leap."

Learning from Wounds

"If we learn from our deepest wounds, they can become our greatest teachers."

Lessons from Adversity

"The most valuable life lessons often come from the most arduous experiences. Our wounds can be the source of the most profound wisdom and growth."

Lessons from Mistakes

"The most valuable life lessons are often the ones learned through our mistakes and failures."

Letting Go

"The howling wind serves as a reminder that we must sometimes let go of things to make room for new things."

Magic of Fairy Tales

"Fairy tales serve as a timeless reminder that there is magic in the world and that, with enough faith, anything is possible."

Manifesting Dreams

"If you can dream it, you have the innate ability to make it a reality in your life."

Mud-Luscious Days

"Mud-luscious days are messy, but they're also full of possibility and growth."

Necessity of Change

"The withering wind may seem harsh and unforgiving, but it is necessary for growth and transformation."

Obstacles as Stepping Stones

"A determined soul sees obstacles as stepping stones to victory, whereas a quitter only sees obstacles."

Paved with Determination

"The road to success is paved with determination, not with the footsteps of quitters."

Power of Dreams

"Don't underestimate the power of your dreams, because they can shape your reality and transform your journey."

Power of Forgiveness

"Hold on to forgiveness, for it frees your heart of resentment and opens the door to healing and peace."

Power of Illumination

"We may appear small and insignificant, like a candle, but our light has the power to warm those around us and illuminate the world."

Power of the Heart

"Never underestimate the power of your heart; it can weather any storm and emerge even stronger."

Prelude of Life

"In the prelude of life, we select the notes of our joys and sorrows, composing a symphony of our own destiny, long before the music of experience begins to play."

Quest for Perfection

"Life's journey is a quest for perfection, where every twist and turn, every challenge faced, weaves into a divine tapestry, harmonising in the grand symphony of our ultimate purpose."

Refusal to Quit

"Quitting may seem like an easy way out, but it will never lead you to the greatness that lies beyond perseverance."

Remember Why

"When you're about to give up, remember why you started. Maintain your focus on your objectives and let perseverance be your guiding force."

Rise from Adversity

"The human spirit, like a phoenix, rises from the ashes of adversity. Scars are not blemishes; they are badges of honour, evidence of battles fought and the indomitable spirit that endured."

Scars Tell Stories

"Every scar has a story to tell, and every wound can provide insight and fortitude."

Seizing Opportunities

"The opportunity window is always open, but it is up to us to decide whether to seize it or let it pass."

Serenity in Adversity

"In the face of adversity, channel your inner peace to remain alert, focused, and unwavering. Your serenity under strain serves as a compass to steer you through the most difficult storms."

Sign of Growth

"The fear of failing is a sign that you are venturing outside of your comfort zone, where true growth and transformation occur."

Strength in Conquest

"As we stand tall and conquer the heights perched on top of the world, we are reminded of our strength and resilience."

Surprises of Life

"Life is full of surprises, but each one provides an opportunity to grow and learn."

Symbolism of Butterflies

"Butterflies symbolise the journey of the soul, reminding us that growth often requires patience, vulnerability, and a willingness to embrace the unknown."

Symphony of Existence

"In the dance of life, joy is the melody, and celebration is the rhythm, and together, they compose the symphony of our existence."

The View from the Summit

"From the summit, we realise that the challenges we faced to get there were well worth it because the view is nothing short of spectacular."

The Weight of Now

"The future is a myth, the past a memory—only this moment breathes. Treat it not as a step, but as the path itself."

Transcending Limits

"Ordinary minds merely exist; extraordinary minds dare to transcend the limits of existence."

Transformation from Wounds

"Don't let your wounds define you. Allow them to mould you into a wiser, more resilient, and more sympathetic version of yourself."

Transient Nature of Life

"Like dust and ashes, life is transient, reminding us to cherish every moment and make the most of it."

Unveiling Inner Treasures

"Our struggles compel us to go deeper, unlock our potential, and discover the inner treasures in the fascinating dance of existence."

Unwritten Power

"The chapters of your greatness are not written by fate, but by the ink of your effort. Turn the page. Pick up the pen. The story begins when you believe it can."

LIFE CHANGING JOURNEY

Virtuoso of Purpose

"In the symphony of success, the virtuoso of unwavering purpose and effort always claims centre stage."

Whispers of Dreams

"Dreams are the whispers of your heart, guiding you towards your true calling and unlocking your vast reservoir of potential."

Wind of Change

"Embrace the wind of change, for it carries the possibilities of new beginnings and seeds of growth."

Discovering Self

Reflections on Identity and Purpose

"In the mirror of introspection, we find the reflection of our true self, and in the journey to understand it, we uncover the purpose that gives our life meaning."

- *Shree Shambav*

Acknowledge our mistakes

"When we can humbly acknowledge our mistakes and learn from them, becoming wiser and stronger, that is when we reach the pinnacle of our glory."

Actions Define

"A person's character is measured not by what they say, but by what they do. Choose to do what is right even when no one is looking."

Adversity's Propulsion

"Adversity is the wind beneath your wings, propelling you higher than you ever imagined. Accept the storm as the catalyst for your ascension."

Alchemy of Willpower

"Within the crucible of desire, the alchemy of willpower transmutes intentions into the golden actions that define your journey."

Architects of Destiny

"Our future joys and sorrows are crafted in the forge of our choices today, for in the realm of destiny, we are the architects of our own emotional tapestry."

Beauty of Reflection

"A beautiful reflection captures both the beauty of our soul and the beauty of our outward appearance."

Belief in Miracles

"Miracles happen every day, but only those who believe in them can see their power."

Blossoming Heart

"In the garden of life, let good feelings bloom within your heart, and watch as they transform into the most beautiful and meaningful actions."

Boundless Potential

"Within every individual resides the boundless expanse of the entire ocean, not merely a solitary drop adrift in the sea of existence."

Choosing Righteousness

"In a world where you can be anything, choose to be someone who always does the right thing."

Connecting with Nature

"I find myself, lose myself, and connect with something greater than myself when I go deep into nature."

Desire for Enlightenment

"Desire the light of life as fervently as you desire each breath, and you will discover the path to enlightenment."

Difficult Times

"The most difficult times in our lives can bring out the best in us, challenging us to discover strength and resilience within ourselves that we may not have known existed."

Digital Labyrinth

"In the intricate maze of social media addiction, the walls are built not of bricks but of endless scrolls, trapping us in a digital labyrinth where the threads of connection blur into the chaos of constant notifications."

Embrace Newness

"If you try nothing new, you'll never know what you're truly capable of."

Embrace the Hustle

"Those who hustle will find success. The keys to achieving greatness are hard work, determination, and perseverance. Don't wait for opportunities to come to you; instead, create them through unwavering perseverance and a never-ending grind. Accept the hustle, and you'll be surprised at what you can achieve."

Embracing Diverse Views

"A heart unwilling to embrace diverse views often discovers a desolate landscape, where agreement is a rare companion."

Emotional Tapestry

"The tapestry of our existence is woven with the threads of our preconceived joys and sorrows, for it is our choices that cast the die of our emotional journey."

Empowering the Mind and Spirit

"The mind awakens when it questions fear, but the spirit rises when it remembers its light. True power is not control—but the quiet clarity that comes when thought and soul walk hand in hand."

Endless Memories

"The journey is over at the end of the road, but the memories will last a lifetime."

Eternal Truth

"A lie, a fleeting illusion in the passing hours, is but a speck in the vast ocean of time." The truth, on the other hand, stands as an eternal lighthouse, guiding us through the storms of existence."

Exploring Emotions

"Exploring inner emotions is akin to deciphering the verses of a sacred text, in which each emotion is a chapter and the heart is the reader. In this profound exploration, we find the keys to understanding both ourselves and the universe."

Exploring the Inner Universe

"Within the depths of one's heart and mind, a universe awaits exploration, filled with limitless possibilities and potential."

Faith's Guardian Knot

"In the boundless expanse of existence, faith emerges as the unbreakable guardian knot, a luminous tether that steadies our souls amidst swirling cosmic currents, igniting a profound, unwavering connection."

Flame of Willpower

"The flame of your willpower burns brightly when fuelled by deep desire, casting the radiant glow of your actions in its warm embrace."

Forgiveness and Love

"You will be happy if you do not pass judgment. You will be happier if you forgive everything. You will be happiest if you love everything."

Fuelling the Soul

"The soul is not fed by noise or applause, but by the silent fire of purpose, the warmth of truth, and the gentle breath of meaning—where even the smallest act, done with love, becomes eternal nourishment."

Generosity vs. Pride

"Generosity tilts the scales of life towards abundance, while pride tilts them away."

Grasping Opportunities

"When presented with an opportunity, grasp it with both hands and give it your all. You never know where your efforts will take you."

Growth from Struggle

"Life's most difficult times often lead to the most beautiful moments of growth and transformation. Embrace the struggle and treasure the lessons learned; they will mould you into the person they always meant you to be."

Guiding Flame

"The flame of beauty burns eternally in the heart, far brighter than any transient outward appearance."

Guiding Light of Hope

"Where there is hope, there is always a way forward. Even in the darkest of times, the light of hope can shine brightly and point us in the direction of a brighter tomorrow."

Heart's Glow

"The most beautiful glow a person can have is the light of their heart."

Hope's Promise

"Where there is hope, there is the possibility of change, growth, healing, and a better tomorrow."

Illusion of Relationships

"We are born alone, live alone, and die alone. We create the illusion of relationship, love, and friendship during the intermittent. A Maya who makes us feel like we're not alone."

Inner Purity

"No external achievement can bring true happiness unless there is inner purity."

Inner Reflection

"A beautiful reflection reflects inner contentment, joy, and peace."

Interplay of Emotions

"In the vast canvas of emotions, sorrow and joy intertwine, creating a masterpiece that paints the portrait of a life well-lived."

Journey of Self-Discovery

"The journey of self-discovery begins with searching deep within ourselves for answers."

Learning from Mistakes

"To err is human; to learn from mistakes is to elevate the human experience to new heights of understanding."

Lessons from Uncertainty

"In the wake of this bewildering revelation, remember that the greatest lessons are born from the depths of uncertainty."

Life's Complexity

"Life, inherently simple, yet relentlessly complicated by our own complexities."

Life's Journey

"I walked on the rough path, slept under giant trees, bathed in sunshine, immersed in moonlight, wondered on twinkling stars, swam in the sea, breezed through wild air, drank sweet nectar, played with butterflies, sang with the birds, and reached heights watching mountains. Each experience was a reminder that life is not just about existing but truly living, and with each discovery, I found a new piece of myself I never knew existed."

Life's Wind

"Life is like the wind; it can be gentle or fierce, but it always changes and propels us forward."

Lost in Social Media

"In the maze of social media addiction, the paths are paved with pixels, and the destination is often a mirage. While we navigate the corridors of carefully manicured perfection, the true self becomes lost in the intricate patterns of virtual validation."

Mastering Self

"Commanding others showcases strength, yet mastering oneself signifies the essence of true power."

Meditative Nature Walks

"Walking alone through nature can be meditative."

Mirrored Beauty

"A beautiful reflection is not only about what we see in the mirror but also about how we see ourselves in the world."

Nature's Depths

"Deep within nature, we discover not only the world's beauty but also the mysteries of our souls."

LIFE CHANGING JOURNEY

Navigating Uncharted Waters

"In the vast expanse of life, we often find ourselves navigating wild, uncharted waters, where adventure and discovery await those who dare to explore."

New Beginnings

"The end of a road is not the end of a journey, but the beginning of a new one."

Past as a Reference

"The past is a point of reference, not a constraint. Learn from it, but don't let it limit your prospects."

Profound Truths of the Heart

"In the quiet chambers of the heart, emotions carve the most profound truths, etching a narrative that transcends words."

Quest for Enlightenment

"In the quest for enlightenment, let your desire for the light of life burn as intensely as the air you breathe."

Radiant Beauty

"True beauty radiates from the heart, illuminating the world with its inner light."

Radiating Positivity

"One that radiates positivity, kindness, and love towards ourselves and others is a beautiful reflection."

Reflections on Identity and Purpose

"I searched the world to find who I am, only to learn—my purpose was never something to chase, but something I was meant to remember. Not in the mirror, but in the quiet places where my soul first learned to whisper its truth."

Resilience in Tough Times

"Though tough times may persist; they are no match for the human spirit's resilience and perseverance. With each new challenge, we become stronger, wiser, and more capable of overcoming the challenges that lie ahead. Tough times do not last, but our ability to overcome them does."

Respect in Beliefs

"Don't pass judgment on how humans communicate with the supreme because everyone has their way of doing things."

Roots of Anger

"In the mind's garden, attachment plants the seeds of desire, and from those desires, the roots of anger begin to grow."

Seeds of Goodness

"Good thoughts sow the seeds of kindness, good words water the garden of compassion, and good intent shines like the sun on the flowers of empathy, yielding the harvest of good actions."

Silence's Secrets

"Silence has secrets to reveal that words could never express because the soul speaks its deepest truths in the stillness."

Silent Depth

"In the silence of solitude, we discover the depth of our emotions, where the heart's whispers resonate louder than any spoken word."

Solace in Nature

"In the embrace of nature's beauty, we find solace, inspiration, and a reminder of our place in the universe."

Soul's Secrets

"My soul's secrets are buried deep within me, awaiting discovery by those who take the time to listen."

Soul's Treasures

"The greatest treasures in life are found not in material possessions, but in the depths of our souls."

Spirit of the Warrior

"A sword is not measured by its size or material but by the skill and spirit of the warrior who wields it. The finest sword is one that cuts through not only flesh but also the darkness within."

Strength in Adversity

"Difficult times may bring us to our knees, but they will never crush our spirit. Because, just as the darkest night must give way to the dawn, our struggles must eventually give way to our strength."

Symphony of Emotions

"Embrace the symphony of your emotions, for within their ebb and flow lies the essence of your journey—each note a testament to the depth of your human experience."

Test of Character

"The true litmus test of character is not avoiding storms, but rising above them, soaring higher with unwavering resilience and determination."

Timeless Essence

"Fairy tales are more than just true; they speak to the timeless essence of our dreams and aspirations, guiding us through the magical realms of imagination."

Tragic Symphony of Thoughts

"Within the chambers of our thoughts, self-doubts and internal conflicts perform a tragic symphony, casting accusations of helplessness, misery, stupidity, and deception upon the stage of our consciousness."

Triumph over Fear

"Our greatest glory is not the absence of fear, but our ability to triumph over it and keep moving forward."

True Essence

"You are not merely who you appear to be; the profound currents of your deepest desires sculpt your true essence."

True Generosity

"In the realm of giving, true generosity means giving abundantly, and in taking, it's the humility of accepting just enough."

Truest Self

"There is a place deep within me where my truest self-dwells, free of fear and doubt."

Unbreakable Spirit

"I am defined not by external circumstances, but by the unbreakable spirit that lives within me."

Uncharted Exploration

"To explore uncharted waters, one must be willing to let go of the safety of the shore."

Uncovering Treasures

"Appearances can be deceiving, but a closer look reveals the genuine gems. It's in the pursuit of understanding that we uncover life's true treasures."

Unearthing True Selves

"Within the labyrinth of our emotions, we unearth the buried treasures of our true selves. To dive deeply is to embrace the shadows and the light, for it is in their interplay that we discover the mosaic of our existence."

Unfold Your Myth

"Your myth serves as a roadmap to your destiny. Follow its winding paths, overcome obstacles, and look forward to the adventure that awaits. Unfold your myth, and you will live the extraordinary life that is rightfully yours."

Unquenchable Light

"Within the depths of my being lies an unquenchable flame, a light that will guide me through the darkest of times."

Unveiling Existence

"In the midst of catastrophe or tribulation, the heart wrestles with profound questions: 'What is my role in this unfolding drama? Why do we find ourselves born into unique circumstances and situations? How do we navigate the diverse states of existence, from poverty to wealth, from health to illness, and from wickedness to virtue?'"

Unveiling Infinite

"Don't hold back; give it your all. Try your hardest, and the world will open in front of you, revealing infinite possibilities."

Unveiling Potential

"Break free from the constraints placed on you by others and embrace the limitless possibilities that exist within you. Unveiling your myth entails a journey of self-discovery and empowerment."

Venturing Beyond

"New vistas await those with the courage to venture beyond the familiar coastline."

Vibrant Threads of Mistakes

"Mistakes are vibrant threads in the tapestry of life, weaving a story of resilience, progress, and eventual success."

Virtuous Journey

"The journey of a virtuous life begins with nurturing the soil of your mind with good thoughts, and as you tend to your inner garden, the fruits of goodness in your actions will ripen with abundance."

Voice of Truth

"Even though the world is full of lies, there is a voice within me that speaks the truth."

Wealth of Generosity

"Give beyond your means, and you'll discover wealth in the abundance of your heart. If you take less than your fair share, you'll discover the hollowness of pride."

Love and Relationships

Nurturing Connections

"In the garden of life, connections are blooming flowers, and nurturing them is the tender touch that allows beauty to flourish."

- *Shree Shambav*

Ageless Friendship

"True friendship is a treasure that gets better with age because it was forged in the crucible of loyalty and trust."

Art of Forgetting

"Crushes flicker like a spark. Affection grows with each passing hour. Love settles like the evening sun. But the art of forgetting takes a lifetime to master."

Barrier vs. Bridge

"Unfortunately, people are erecting massive barriers around themselves rather than erecting beautiful bridges to connect."

Beautiful Friendship

"In the garden of life, friends are the most beautiful and rarest of flowers, blooming with laughter and nurturing each other's souls."

Beauty in Diversity

"The diversity of religions in our world makes it beautiful; each one is a delicate flower in the garden of human spirituality."

Beauty of Shared Sunsets

"The sunsets we experience with people we care about are the most beautiful."

Blooms of Memory

"In the garden of friendship, the loss of a dear friend is like a withered flower, but their essence continues to bloom in the memories we hold dear."

Bright Stars of Friendship

"Like stars in the night sky, friends brighten our darkest moments and remind us that we're never alone in the vast universe of life."

Bringing Sunshine

"Those who bring sunshine into the lives of others cannot keep it hidden from themselves."

Building Bonds

"We build a beautiful relationship with love, trust, and respect."

Building Bridges of Connection

"It's unfortunate that people are erecting massive barriers around themselves rather than erecting beautiful bridges to connect."

Burden Without Love

"Living is a burden without the sweet life of love."

Celebrating Ordinary Joys

"Celebrate the ordinary moments because they reflect the extraordinary beauty of life, and joy is the art of discovering wonder in the ordinary."

Character's Radiance

"The truest measure of a person's character is their ability to bring sunshine and warmth into the lives of those around them."

Cherished Memories of Friendship

"Losing a friend is like closing a cherished book, but the pages of their impact on our lives remain eternally open in our hearts."

Choice Between Life and Love

"In that moment of choice, you'll ask, 'Life or love?' My answer: 'Life,' not realising you are my entire world."

Contrasting Counsel of Love and Wisdom

"Wisdom may counsel caution with its whispered 'Be careful,' but love, with its exuberant heart, joyfully encourages, 'Dive in and embrace the depths!'"

Cornerstone of Friendship

"A true friend is the cornerstone of a life built on the bedrock of shared values, offering a hand to hold in today's storms and a beacon of hope for tomorrow's horizons."

Embodiment of Motherhood

"In the lexicon of life, 'Mother' is not just a word; it's the embodiment of the purest emotions and the sweetest lullabies."

Embracing Solitude

"Sometimes you need to disconnect from everything and spend some time alone to experience, value, and embrace who you are."

Embracing True Worth

"Value the person for who they are, not for what they can do for you. True worth is found in their character rather than their accomplishments."

Emotional Compass

"Emotions are the heart's compass, guiding us through the uncharted waters of existence. Exploring their depths is a journey of self-discovery in which we unearth the pearls of our innermost feelings."

Eternal Essence of Love

"Love is a profound soul dance in which the steps of separation only add to the grace of reunion. To set a love free, to let it soar, to let it be, is to discover the essence of love's eternity."

Eternal Flame of Love

"Amid life's uncertainties, the mystery of love remains a constant, an eternal flame that lights our path."

Eternal Flame of Mother's Love

"A mother's love, an eternal flame that lights the path of our existence, casting away the shadows with boundless grace."

Eternal Youth

"A soul entwined with the essence of nature remains forever young, for the heart that beats in harmony with the world never wearies in the pursuit of beauty."

Father's Love

"Father's love, like a gentle breeze, may be intangible, but its presence can be felt in every aspect of our existence."

Fleeting Moments

"The fleeting moments bring attraction, the passing hours bring affection, and the days bring love's embrace. Yet, forgetting someone takes a lifetime."

Fleeting Relationships

"Like the fragile dew on leaves, relationships are fleeting and delicate. Handle them with care, or they might vanish with the morning sun."

Flowing Love of Mothers

"A mother's love flows like water, visible and tangible, quenching our every thirst with care and tenderness."

Flowing Relationship

"The most beautiful relationship is one that just flows, no matter what obstacles are in the way."

Focus on Meaning

"Like wind-borne dust, let go of the trivial and focus on what truly matters. In your wake, leave a trail of meaningful ashes."

Foundations of Connection

"The foundations of a genuine relationship are trust, honesty, communication, and mutual respect, which are the pillars of a true relationship."

Foundations of a True Relationship

"Trust, communication, and a willingness to grow together indefinitely, which are the pillars of a genuine relationship, are the foundations of a true relationship."

Fragile Nature of Relationships

"Relationships are like the dew on leaves, fragile and delicate. They require care and attention, or they will evaporate into thin air."

Fuel for Resolve

"When one door of happiness closes, use the experience as fuel to rekindle your resolve and seek new doors that align with your true desires."

Graceful Dance of Relationships

"A beautiful relationship is like a dance; both partners move in perfect harmony, creating something graceful and breathtaking."

Guardian Angel Friend

"A friend is like a guardian angel who lifts you when your wings forget how to fly and carries you through life's challenges with unwavering support."

Guiding Light

"A friend is a lighthouse that guides you through life's choppy waters by illuminating your path with love and understanding."

Guiding Light of Mothers

"Mothers are the heartbeat of our lives, the ones who guide us through the ups and downs, and the light that shines even in the darkest moments."

Guru's Illumination

"A Guru is a teacher, guide, and mentor who illuminates the path to knowledge, wisdom, and self-realisation."

Guru's Remembrance

"A Guru is someone who helps you remember what you have forgotten, not someone who teaches you something new."

Harmonious Refrain of Motherhood

"The word 'Mother' echoes with the gentle hum of love, a harmonious refrain that binds hearts and souls together in the most beautiful melody of existence."

Healing Grips

"The pain of losing someone close to your heart is like a grip that refuses to let go. It leaves you with an ache that only time and memories can heal."

Healing Hearts

"When broken hearts unite, they may still bear the scars of past pain, but together they can find the courage to love again and the strength to heal."

Illuminate the Night

"A candle's light may flicker and dim, but it never loses its ability to illuminate the darkness and bring warmth to the coldest of nights."

Impactful Happiness

"The ability to positively impact the lives of others is a true measure of happiness. If you can't make others happy, seek to understand and grow."

Inspiring Goodness in Others

"If you train your eyes to see the good in others, you will inspire them to see the good in themselves."

Interconnected Particles

"We are all interconnected, like particles of dust and ashes, a reminder that our actions ripple through time and affect the world around us."

Interwoven Bonds

"In the tapestry of life, a true friend is a thread that weaves together our past, present, and future, creating a story of shared principles and enduring bonds."

Journey of the Heart

"The heart's journey is a maze of options through which love's true essence emerges. Letting go opens the door to self-discovery, and if destiny binds two souls together, they will reunite stronger and forever changed."

Kindness Option

"In a world where kindness is an option, if you can't embrace it, at least refrain from causing harm to other living beings."

Life Defined by Loved Ones

"When I chose my life over yours, little did you know, you had already become my life."

Living Fairy Tales

"In the realm of fairy tales, reality and fantasy collide, revealing profound truths about the human spirit. These tales come alive in the hearts of dreamers and shape our destinies."

Love's Cartography

"Love is a map to an uncharted realm, where the journey is just as captivating as the destination."

Love's Enduring Ink

"In the book of our hearts, love is written with the ink of a lifetime."

Love's Intricate Weaving

"In the tapestry of love, the threads of freedom and trust are woven with as much tenderness as the threads of attachment. If love is meant to be, it will return stronger and more lovely than before."

Meaningful Life with Loved Ones

"When faced with that question, my reply may be 'my life,' but you'll never know. It's you who gives my life meaning."

Mother's Endless Embrace

"In the vastness of a mother's love, like water, we find solace, nourishment, and unwavering support."

Mysterious Nature of Love

"When you're in love, there's no need to understand what's going on, because everything happens inside of you."

Mystery of Love

"Love's mystery lies not in its answers, but in the questions that lead us on a lifelong journey of discovery."

Nature's Embrace

"In the embrace of nature's love, a man finds the elixir of eternal youth, and his spirit forever dances with the timeless rhythm of the Earth."

Nurturing Connections

"Nurturing connections is like tending to a flame in the heart; they cast a warm and comforting glow that lights our path in the darkest of times."

Nurturing Marriage

"Marriage is a garden that requires constant nurturing and care, but it can blossom into a beautiful and everlasting love with patience and dedication."

Painful Reminders

"The pain of losing a friend is like a tear in the fabric of our heart, a reminder of the beautiful threads of connection that once bound us."

Parental Shelter

"In the tempest of life, a parent's sacrifice is a protective embrace, safeguarding their cherished ones."

Path to Happiness

"The key to finding happiness is selflessness. When you make it your mission to make others happy, you open the door to your inner joy."

Pillars of Trust

"A true relationship is built on trust, mutual respect, and a willingness to always be there for each other, through both good times and bad."

Precious Currency of Love

"Love is the most precious currency; invest it wisely, and the returns will be immeasurable."

Precious Gift of Understanding

"Understanding is the most precious gift of love, for it illuminates the heart's depths and weaves the tapestry of connections that bind souls together."

Prioritise Love Over Money

"Prioritise love over money, for love enriches the soul and brings true fulfilment that no amount of wealth can provide."

Profound Offering of Comprehension

"Comprehension stands as love's most profound offering, as it unlocks the heart's gateway to the intricate beauty of another's soul."

Profound Silence

"The profound beauty of love lies not in the words uttered, but in the emotions unsurfaced, in the profound silence where hearts converse without the need for spoken language."

Realities of Fairy Tales

"Beyond the pages of storybooks, fairy tales become a manifestation of our deepest hopes and desires, proving that reality can be as captivating as fiction."

Resonance of Emotions

"The resonance of one person's suffering reverberates within us all, while the glow of one person's happiness becomes a collective celebration."

Revelation of True Intentions

"Words are only a pretext; actions reveal a person's true intentions and character."

Seeds of Compassion

"Helping the needy in their time of despair is sowing compassion seeds that will one day blossom into the support you seek in your hour of need."

Sharing Happiness

"Happy experiences can be shared. By bringing joy to those around you, you create a nurturing environment in which your happiness can flourish."

Shelter of Hearts

"Let us seek the shelter of hearts where love endures throughout the journey of life, for there lies our greatest treasure."

Siblings' Bond

"There can be no better companion than a brother and no better friend than a sister."

Silent Anchors

"Just as air sustains life, a father's love silently anchors us, giving strength to our roots and lifting us towards the skies."

Silent Longings

"Lost in the translation of unspoken sentiments, love often lingers in the silent pauses, yearning for the language of the heart to be truly heard."

Singing Freedom

"Sing like a bird, for beauty lies in expressing yourself without regard for judgement or opinions."

Solace in Enduring Love

"Amidst the storms of life, I find solace in a place where your love endures."

Soul's Palette

"Emotions are the soul's palette, painting our lives with hues of passion, tenderness, and resilience. Exploring their depths reveals the raw, unadulterated beauty of our human spirit."

Strength in Adversity

"Relationships glisten not by holding hands in good times, but rather by firmly holding hands in bad times."

Substance Over Eloquence

"Don't be deceived by eloquent words; they can be a mere pretext concealing a lack of substance."

The Paradox of Love

"Love is a lovely paradox in which freedom and attachment coexist. When you set someone free and they choose to return, their love is a precious gift that was always meant for you."

Transcendent Connections

"Our connections transcend space and time, tying us to the eternal dance of the universe, from the depths of our souls to the farthest reaches of the cosmos."

Treasures of Bonds

"In the treasure troves of life, it's the beauty of bonds that transcends wealth and possessions."

Triumph of Love

"Wisdom may entangle in knots of complexity and peril, yet love triumphs, breaking through every boundary and danger."

True Friendship Measure

"True friendship assesses the durability of bonds over time rather than the number of days, months, or years."

True Riches of Love

"Money is a powerful tool, but it should never be allowed to overshadow the true riches of love and connection."

Ultimate Act of Trust

"In the ebb and flow of love, setting someone free is the ultimate act of trust. It's the fine line that separates fated love from fleeting love."

Unconstrained Love

"Love is about connection, not possession. Releasing someone you care about is a profound acknowledgement that their happiness and yours are inextricably linked but never constrained."

Unspoken Truths of Love

"Sometimes, the depth of love lies in the unspoken truths, where my life is yours, and yours is mine."

Unspoken Verses of Love

"In the unspoken silences, love writes its most profound verses, weaving emotions between the words left unsaid."

Unwavering Love of Mothers

"Just as the storm rages on, a mother's love never wavers, ensuring her nest remains safe from harm."

Vibrant Threads of Friendship

"In the tapestry of life, friends are vibrant threads that add colour, strength, and warmth to the canvas of our existence."

Wealth of Love

"The greatest wealth is found in an abundance of love and the freedom to live life on your terms."

Finding Inner Strength
Empowering the Mind and Spirit

"Empowering the mind and spirit is the journey to free ourselves from the shackles of limitation, allowing us to soar on the wings of our potential."

- *Shree Shambav*

Abandoning Gates to Self-Destruction

"The three gates of hell that lead to the abyss of self-destruction for the soul are greed, anger, and lust. As a result, all three should be abandoned."

Alchemy of Greatness

"The alchemy of greatness was discovered in the crucible of passion and the spark of enthusiasm. These are the vital fuels that ignite the fire within us, propelling us inexorably towards the fulfilment of our dreams and aspirations."

Anxiety and Future Reins

"Anxiety finds its roots in our relentless desire to hold the reins of the future, not in the uncertainty it holds."

Anxiety's Origin

"The source of our anxiety lies not in the mysteries of tomorrow, but in our unending quest to master it."

Butterflies and New Beginnings

"Butterflies gracefully emerge from their cocoons, spreading their wings and welcoming a new beginning, reminding us that transformation is possible."

Canvas of True Freedom

"True freedom is the canvas on which human dignity is painted; it is a place where rights are honoured, voices are heard, and the spirit soars free of the shackles of oppression."

Choosing Righteousness over Convenience

"The world is full of people who do what is easiest or most convenient, but the world needs more people who do what is right."

Choosing the Right Path

"When confronted with a hard choice, ask yourself, 'what is the right thing to do?' And then, no matter what, do it."

Clarity in Thought

"Never let your thoughts be cluttered as in troubled waters, because it is difficult to see through murky and hazy water. Instead, cultivate an attitude of a fresh running stream, and your perceptions will be crystal clear."

Courage to Set Sail

"You can't just stare out at the sea and expect to cross it. To set sail, one must have the courage to face the waves and a steadfast heart to reach the other shore."

Discovery of True Wealth

"A true beggar is unable to discover his true wealth."

Distinguishing Fame from Glory

"Fame may shine brightly, but glory enlightens the soul and leaves a lasting impression."

Dive Deep with Courage

"Dive deep, not just with ambition, but with a heart brimming with courage, and you'll bring to shore the pearls of profound emotions."

Divine Harmony of Music

"Music is a divine means of connecting with the soul, healing the heart, and elevating the spirit."

Doing the Right Thing

"Doing the right thing is not a matter of convenience; it reflects your values and integrity."

Don't confuse

"Don't confuse fame with glory; one is fleeting, while the other endures beyond the spotlight."

Earth's Garden

"The Earth is a garden; it is a wonderful place for all living things, including the human race."

Embrace Your Myth

"Do not be afraid to unravel the layers of your being and delve into the depths of your potential. Embrace your myth, for it contains the power to change how you live."

Embracing New Horizons

"Only by letting go of the familiar shore can you embark on the voyage to new horizons."

Embracing the Flow of Life

"Like a river's meandering course, go easy in the flow of life—embracing tranquilly, nurturing growth, and allowing the beauty of the journey to unfold."

Embracing the Present

"Embracing the present, with all its facets, is the first step towards crafting a future steeped in transformation and possibility."

Embracing the Unknown of the Sea

"Those who fear the sea's vastness remain unconquered. To cross it, one must embrace the unknown, channel their inner strength, and face the challenges with unwavering resolve."

Expectations and Reliance

"Like intertwined vines, expectations give birth to reliance, and in the shadow of that reliance, burdens and entanglements take root."

Faith in the Tapestry of Existence

"In the vast tapestry of existence, faith stands as an unbreakable guardian knot that anchors our souls, weaving our deepest emotions into the very fabric of reality."

Fuelling the Inferno Within

"Without the furnace of passion and the flame of enthusiasm, I've forged nothing extraordinary. They are the powerful forces that fuel the inferno within us, propelling us relentlessly towards the fulfilment of our dreams and goals."

Guidance of "Go Easy"

"Let 'go easy' be your compass on your journey of moments, guiding you with kindness and wisdom through the tides of time."

Guiding Light of Faith

"He who led you this far will not forsake you now."

Heaven and Hell in the Present

"In the tapestry of now, heaven and hell unfold, woven into the present moment. Stop worrying about distant heavens and embrace the knowledge that they coexist in the present."

Idealism Leading to Righteousness

"Being idealistic and seeking what is right will only lead us towards the right goal. Our valuable life needs to trust the right way to serve dispassionately in an unattached manner."

Igniting the Spark of Hope

"We muster the courage to ignite the spark that will bring us back to the light when things seem hopeless."

Impact of Attachment on Yearning

"The yearning that you experience repeatedly is the way your mind is attached. When a desire is sparked, there are two outcomes: fulfilment leads to greed, and unfulfillment leads to sorrow, rage, and misery."

Indelible Marks of Moments

"Even though puddle-wonderful moments are fleeting, they leave an indelible mark on our hearts and souls."

Influence of Perspective on Perception

"What you see is influenced not only by what you look at, but also by where you look deeply. The things you look at change as you change your perspective about them."

Inner Flame of Beauty

"In the profound tapestry of existence, beauty is not a mere reflection in the mirror, but a luminous flame ignited deep within the chambers of the heart."

Inspiring Hearts, Not Fleeting Fame

"Glory resides in the hearts of those you inspire, not in fleeting moments of fame."

Instinctive Reactions vs. Natural Flow

"Reactions are always instinctive; never turn yourself into restless water by reacting immediately. Be like a fresh, flowing, gleeful stream. We realise that as we develop in a natural sense in the diverse environment, these values are internalised and practised in our life like the ever-flowing stream."

Interconnectedness of Freedom

"Who is bound to whom? Is the cow tethered to this man, or is the man tethered to the cow?"

Lessons from Butterflies

"Butterflies teach us about the beauty of change and the freedom that comes from letting go of what no longer serves us."

Life's Ceaseless River

"Life is a river, flowing ceaselessly through the unreal world until it merges with the eternal sea of existence."

Living a Life of Integrity

"Doing the right thing is about living a life of integrity and honour, not seeking praise or recognition."

Logical Minds or Illogical Perception

"We all think our minds are very logical, but I perceive them to be very illogical."

Measuring True Glory

"Glory is measured not by the number of followers or the ovations of the crowd, but by the impact and difference you make."

Mind's Creation of Reality

"The mind can create a heaven of hell as well as a hell of heaven."

Nurturing Expectations

"Expectations are the seeds that nurture the growth of reliance in the garden of life; however, if left unchecked, this reliance may blossom into the heavy flowers of burden and the intricate vines of entanglement."

Perception of Truth by Soul's Inner Eye

"The soul's inner eye perceives the truth beyond appearances, unlocking the power of intuition and wisdom."

Philosophy of Living in the Present

"The best philosophy is to live in the present moment, with gratitude for the past and hope for the future, while making the most of each day."

Plagued Minds

"Our minds, incessantly plagued by self-doubts and internal conflicts, often accuse us of helplessness, misery, foolishness, and deception."

Portal to the Soul

"The inner eye of the soul is the portal to our deepest selves, where our true purpose and destiny reside."

Positive Impact on the Environment

"Our actions in the environment can have a positive impact. We can affect change by acting morally."

Power of Now

"The past is merely a memory, and the future is only a projection. The true source of now is always accessible, right here and right now. Accept it, because it has the power to shape your reality."

Principle of Doing the Right Thing

"Doing the right thing is never easy, but it is always the right thing to do."

Principle over Convenience

"Doing the right thing is a matter of principle, not convenience or circumstance."

Puddle-Wonderful Surprises

"Life is full of puddle-wonderful surprises, we just have to open our eyes and be willing to see them."

Release of Uninteresting Burdens

"We carry a lot of things that do not interest us, and we strive to control them."

Restless Minds

"Our mind is like a monkey and will not stay in one place."

Silent Canvas of Suffering

"In the depths of suffering, silence becomes a canvas upon which each heart paints its pain."

Soul's Symphony in Solitude

"While in pain, the soul withdraws into solitude, where its agony transforms into an ethereal symphony that only it can hear."

Speed of Consciousness

"Life is changing at the speed of consciousness, awareness, and change, and man no longer confines or accepts destiny; but applies his potential mind to question the complexities of life and the causes of events."

Standing Alone for Righteousness

"Doing the right thing sometimes means standing up for what we believe in, even if it means standing alone."

Strength in Exploring Uncharted Waters

"You find the strength to explore uncharted waters in the courage to lose sight of the coast."

Symphony of Individuality in Freedom

"The world of freedom contains the symphony of individuality. It produces a melody that, like distinct notes coming together, resonates with the essence of human potential."

The Farmer's Embrace

"The farmer's embrace of the land is an embrace of life itself. Each furrow ploughed, each seed sown, encapsulates a saga of resilience, echoing the whispers of ancestors and promising a legacy of sustenance, hard-earned and well-deserved."

The Farmer's Testament

"Among the golden fields, the farmer stands as a testament to the indomitable spirit. Their unwavering efforts, like a symphony performed in concert with the elements, resonate with the echoes of generations past and dreams for the future."

The Light Beneath Loss

"Loss does not erase love—it reveals its depth. Grief is love that has lost its destination but not its devotion."

The Weight of Anxiety

"The weight of anxiety comes from our indomitable desire to shape the future, not from the unknown future."

Tranquil Mind's Direction

"Your mind is like troubled waters; when it is disturbed or agitated, allow it to settle, and they will perceive it in the right direction on its own."

Transformation of the Caterpillar

"Just as the caterpillar thought the world was coming to an end, it transformed into a butterfly, symbolising the power of resilience and growth."

Transformative Power of Puddles

"Puddles may appear insignificant, but they have the power to transform a mundane day into something magical."

Transient Aspirations

"Many aspire to a higher or more fulfilling life, but the seeking is usually only an impulse of the moment, unrealised and not sustained."

True Beauty Beyond the Surface

"Look beyond the surface, for true beauty emanates not from the face but from the radiant light that dwells within the heart."

True Freedom from Emotional Servitude

"Servitude to one's likes and dislikes is servitude to one's emotions. True freedom comes from refusing to become attached to or bound by any form, object, situation, or activity."

True Glory Beyond Fame

"Fame may bring attention, but true glory is earned through meaningful actions and genuine contributions."

Uncovering Life's Alchemy

"Souls, like salt and camphor, may appear to be similar on the surface, but the alchemy of life carves each with a distinct essence. Accept the path of uncovering, for it contains the enchantment of finding life's hidden complexities."

Universal Emotions

"Isn't it true that all living beings have the same emotions as humans do?"

Unwavering Spirit Overcoming Obstacles

"Never give up because you have an unwavering spirit that can overcome any obstacle within you. Continue forward and believe in yourself."

LIFE CHANGING JOURNEY

Embracing Imperfections

Embracing Self-Acceptance

"Self-acceptance is the gentle rain that nourishes the roots of our worth and enables us to bloom with the beauty of our truth."

- Shree Shambav

Appreciating Life's Gifts

"Learn to appreciate the gifts that life bestows on you because they serve as the foundation for your unique journey."

Architect of Your Life

"You are the architect of your own life. Each day is a new canvas and every choice you make is a stroke of the brush. Create your masterpiece one day at a time, and never be afraid to try new things or take chances. Your life is your own, and it is up to you to make it a work of art."

Authenticity of Unspoken Thoughts

"We find the true canvas of another's reality in the unspoken. The silent symphony of their unspoken thoughts paints a more profound portrait than words could ever do."

Bravery in Risk-Taking

"While going down in flames is painful, it demonstrates your bravery and willingness to take risks."

Burning Brighter After Flames

"When everything seems to be lost and you're on the verge of burning out, remember that sometimes you have to go down in flames to light the way for a brighter future."

Carrying Joy

"Carrying joy in your heart allows you to find beauty in the most unexpected places, turning ordinary moments into cherished memories."

Caution in Desires

"The hues of attachment are painted on the canvas of human emotions, giving rise to desires that bloom like flowers. Yet, be wary, for beneath these cravings lie dormant seeds of rage, waiting for the right moment to sprout."

Celebrating Self

"Celebrate yourself and honour the fact that you are your best thing, a unique and irreplaceable expression of life."

Cherishing Impermanence

"Life's transience is a poignant reminder that every moment is a treasure, every step a fleeting journey, and every embrace a temporary solace. We find the beauty of cherishing what we have in its impermanence, for it is with time that we discover the true value of each heartbeat."

Cultivating Joy

"Joy is not a destination; it is a state of mind that we cultivate through gratitude, mindfulness, and keeping an open heart to the wonders of life."

Daring Pursuit of Dreams

"Going down in flames is not a sign of failure, but that you dared to push boundaries and pursue your dreams with unwavering passion."

Defining Moments

"What defines us is not the circumstances we face, but how we respond to them. We are defined by our character, our resilience, and our ability to rise above adversity. No matter what life throws our way, we have the power to choose how we will respond and the strength to overcome any challenge."

Discovering Inner Strength

"The journey through wild, uncharted waters tests our mettle, but it's in these uncharted depths that we uncover our true strength and resilience."

Discovering Truth in Darkness

"When things are at their darkest, we discover our deepest truths and create a stronger version of ourselves."

Embrace Authenticity

"Hold on to your authenticity, for it is what makes you unique and allows you to shine your light in the world."

Embracing Adversity

"Faced with adversity, embrace the flames that threaten to consume you, for it is only in the fire that you will find the strength to reinvent yourself."

Embracing Life's Challenges

"It's not the circumstances of our lives that define us, but how we choose to respond to them. Our character and strength are forged in the challenges we face and the decisions we make. Embrace life's difficulties as opportunities for growth and never give up on what truly matters to you."

Embracing Mistakes

"Embrace mistakes as essential lessons on life's journey; they are the stepping stones to growth and wisdom."

Embracing Moments of Stillness

"In the embrace of moments of stillness, we discover that silence is not an absence, but a presence—an invitation to listen to our soul's whispers and the secrets of the universe."

Embracing Mysteries

"Embrace the mysteries that emerge in the wake of perplexing revelations; they hold the keys to your growth."

Embracing Self-Acceptance

"Embrace your flaws, your strengths, and every aspect of your being, because it is only through self-acceptance that you can truly become your best self."

Embracing Self-Worth

"Embrace the truth that you are your best thing, for within you lie immeasurable worth and potential."

Embracing Stillness

"Embracing moments of stillness is akin to sipping from the cup of eternity, where time stands still, and we become one with the universe. It is in these pauses that we find the deepest truths and the greatest clarity."

Endurance of Pain

"The endurance of pain is not the end, but the beginning of a journey into the uncharted territories of our own resilience and profound existence."

Endurance of Truth

"The lifespan of a lie may be fleeting, lasting only a few hours, but the endurance of truth stretches across the expanse of eternity."

Every Step Counts

"The journey of a thousand miles starts with a single step. Don't wait for the perfect moment, the perfect conditions, or the perfect plan. Start where you are, with what you have, and take the first step towards your dreams. Every step counts, no matter how small."

Finding Strength in Challenges

"Sometimes, life's gifts come wrapped in challenges, but within those challenges lies the opportunity to find strength and resilience."

Giving Your All

"Give it your all, because greatness awaits those who rise to the occasion with unwavering determination."

Going the Extra Mile

"Go the extra mile. The difference between average and exceptional is just a little extra effort. Put in the work and go above and beyond what is expected of you, and you will see the rewards of your labour. Don't settle for mediocrity; strive for excellence and leave a lasting impact."

Gratitude as a Bridge

"When appreciation seems distant, let gratitude be the bridge that connects hearts."

Growth in Darkness

"Within the depths of darkness lies the potential for profound growth and transformation, because it is in the shadows that we discover our true essence."

Guidance of Values

"Hold fast to your values, for they are the compass that guides your actions and shapes your character."

Holding onto Dreams

"Hold on to your dreams, because they are the blueprints for your future and the source of inspiration that fuels your journey."

Holding onto Faith

"Hold on to your faith, for it is the anchor that keeps you steady amidst the uncertainties of life and gives you the courage to face challenges."

Holding onto Gratitude

"Hold on to gratitude, for it reminds you of the blessings in your life and helps you cultivate a positive perspective."

Holding onto Hope

"Hold onto hope, because it is the fuel that ignites dreams and propels us forward in the face of adversity."

Holding onto Inner Strength

"Hold onto your inner strength, because it is the foundation upon which you can weather any storm and emerge stronger than before."

Holding onto Love

"Hold onto love, because it is the greatest gift we can give and receive, and it has the power to heal and transform lives."

Holding onto Passions

"Hold on to your passions, for they are the sparks that ignite your soul and give purpose to your existence."

Inner Light in Darkness

"On the canvas of our darkest moments, our inner light paints its most vivid colours."

Internal Reflection

"Everything you gaze upon, be it the things you cherish or those you scorn, exists within you to varying degrees."

Joy's Contagious Nature

"When you have joy in your heart, it becomes contagious, spreading its light to everyone you meet."

Learning from Mistakes

"Mistakes serve as a reminder that life's canvas is not perfect, but it's the imperfections that make it a masterpiece worth cherishing."

Life as a Masterpiece

"Your life is your masterpiece, and you are the artist. Every experience, every decision, every moment is an opportunity to create something beautiful and meaningful. So, take control of the brush, and paint the picture you want for your life. Make it a masterpiece that reflects your passions, your values, and your dreams."

Life's Unexpected Gifts

"Life's gifts may appear in unexpected forms but always contain priceless lessons and life-changing experiences."

Making the Most of Life

"Do what you can with what you have, where you are. Life is a journey, and sometimes it can be overwhelming, but it's important to remember that you have the power to make a difference in your own life and the lives of those around you. Use what you have, work with what you've got, and always strive to do your best."

Mindset and Joy

"Embrace the truth that joy does not happen to us; it reflects our mindset and choices."

Moving Past Shadows

"Let the shadows fall behind you. As you move forward and pursue your dreams, don't let your fears and doubts hold you back. Keep your eyes fixed on your goals and let your confidence and determination guide you. The shadows may linger for a time, but with persistence and perseverance, they will eventually fade into the distance."

Natural Positivity

"When joy becomes a natural part of who you are, positivity and abundance will easily flow into your life."

Passion and Greatness

"Wholehearted passion gives birth to greatness - half-heartedness breeds mediocrity."

Perception of Beauty

"An optimist is enthralled by the beauty of a lotus flower that has grown from filth and is clean and pure, whereas a pessimist is concerned about the filth it grew from and cannot recognise the beauty that has emerged."

Readiness for Transformation

"It's never too late to introspect and ask, 'Am I prepared for a transformative journey? Can I evolve from within?'"

Recognising Self-Worth

"You can define your worth and chart your course. Never lose sight of the fact that you are your best asset."

Rediscovering Stillness

"Amidst the chaos of life's relentless rhythm, stillness is the sanctuary where we rediscover our inner compass, aligning ourselves with the essence of our being and the cadence of existence."

Refreshment in Nature

"Getting your hands in the soil can be relaxing. Because of the fresh air and new ideas, you'll feel more energised."

Revitalisation and Rebirth

"At every heartbeat and with every new breath, one should experience revitalisation and rebirth."

Rise Beyond the Shell

"You are not your limitations. You are the space between your fear and your becoming—the crack where light dares to enter and transform."

Shaping by Life's Offerings

"Life's offerings may not always align with your expectations, but they are tailor-made to shape you into the person you were meant to be."

Solitude for Self-Reflection

"Solitude is the choice to be alone for self-reflection and happiness."

Starting the Journey

"It doesn't matter where you start, what's important is that you start. Every journey begins with a single step, so take that step today and start pursuing your dreams. No matter where you are in life, it's never too late to begin creating the future you want."

Stone's Wisdom

"A mountain does not rush to grow, nor a forest race to rise—yet they endure, not through force, but by being wholly themselves. So too, the soul must learn the art of grounded becoming."

Transformation in Adversity

"Don't be afraid to go down in flames, because it is often in the ashes that you find the seeds of transformation and growth."

Understanding Oneself

"In the symphony of life, comprehending others is an intellectual note, but finding the melody within oneself is the sublime wisdom that resonates with the soul."

Understanding Others

"To understand another, delve into the unspoken realms, for there, in the silence, you'll find the authentic tapestry of their existence."

Wisdom of Self-Discovery

"Discerning others is a testament to intelligence, but unravelling the intricacies of oneself is the embodiment of true wisdom."

Gratitude and Mindfulness

Finding Joy in the Present

"In the garden of now, joy is the vibrant bloom we pluck, its fragrance a reminder that life's beauty is woven into each passing moment."

- Shree Shambav

Age as Fortitude

"Age is not a barrier; rather, it represents fortitude and the power of the human spirit. At any age, you can still make a difference, so live each day with passion and purpose."

Best Philosophy

"The best philosophy is to live in the present moment, learn from the past, and look forward with an open mind and heart."

Bringing Sunshine

"In a world that can sometimes be clouded by darkness, be the person who brings sunshine into the lives of others, and watch as your own life becomes brighter in return."

Celebrating Challenges

"'Dancing in the Rains' is a celebration of embracing life's challenges and finding beauty in every moment, no matter what the circumstances."

Celebrating Humanity's Tapestry

"We celebrate the tapestry of humanity in poems about love, diversity, and connection, where every thread is a unique soul, and every stitch is a testament to the beauty of our shared existence."

Choosing Happiness

"Life is a collection of moments, and choosing to be happy in each one can create a lifetime of fulfilment."

Choosing Joy

"Joy is a conscious choice to celebrate the surrounding blessings, to find beauty in everyday life, and to appreciate the present moment."

Clarity at the Summit

"On top of the world, we gain newfound clarity, as the vastness of the landscape mirrors the vastness of our potential."

Connection at the Summit

"From the highest peak, we can reach out and touch the sky, feeling a profound connection to the universe, and experiencing a sense of awe and wonder."

Continuous Exploration

"Dwelling means missing out on the wonders that await. Continue to move, explore, and let your journey unfold."

Cultivating Inner Joy

"Don't rely on external circumstances to bring you joy; cultivate it from within and allow it to pervade all aspects of your life."

Dance of Joy in Rain

"The raindrops falling from the sky are an invitation to let go of your inhibitions and dance with unabashed joy and freedom."

Depth of Love's Enigma

"Love, an enigma, reveals the profundity of its depths only in the heartbreaking hour of separation. The heart discovers the vastness of its own capacity to love in the echoes of absence."

Discovering Bliss in Nature

"One can discover true bliss in nature's stillness."

Doubt as Fuel for Determination

"Let doubt be a spark that ignites the fire of determination, not a storm that extinguishes the flames of your dreams."

Earth's Odes

"The Earth's odes are written in nature's language, sung by the birds, and painted in the colours of the seasons, a love song to the planet we call home."

Embrace Happiness Now

"Don't let the fleeting nature of time overshadow the opportunity to be happy at this very moment."

Embrace the Wisdom of Age

"Embrace the knowledge and experience that comes with age, and use it to fuel your determination to continue breaking down barriers and reaching new heights."

Embracing Fear

"Fear of failure is often a sign that something extraordinary is about to happen. Accept the unknown and believe in your strength."

Embracing Happiness

"Embrace happiness wholeheartedly, and watch as your smile turns into a beacon of light, bringing joy to all who see it."

Embracing Impermanence

"Time dances to its rhythm, and as the sun sets on every life, let us embrace the beauty of impermanence."

Embracing the Present Moment

"Let go of expectations and embrace the present moment with an open heart and a curious mind to unlock the joy within you."

Endless Opportunities for Reinvention

"You can always reinvent yourself, learn new skills, and embrace the endless opportunities that lie ahead of you."

Enjoy the Wonderful Present

"Stop worrying about the past or the future, and just enjoy this wonderful time right now."

Enriching Small Moments

"Small moments of laughter, gratitude, and connection truly enrich our lives, so choose to bring joy into your life every day."

Essence of Nature

"Deep within nature lies the essence of life, where the world's beauty reveals itself in its purest form, and the soul finds solace in Mother Earth's serene embrace."

Ever-changing Tapestry of Existence

"In the ever-changing tapestry of existence, life's transience is the thread that weaves moments into memories, experiences into wisdom, and presence into a profound legacy. We learn to dance gracefully through the seasons of our lives, finding solace in the awareness that even in ends, there is the promise of new beginnings."

Every Being a Work of Art

"Every living being and element in nature is a work of art that contributes to life's grand symphony."

Freedom in Expression

"Find solace in singing like the birds, for their music is free of expectations and criticism. Allow your voice to be heard."

Freedom to Create Joy

"When one happiness door closes, let go of attachments and embrace the freedom to create your joy, unlocking the infinite possibilities that lie before you."

Gratitude and Mindfulness

"Gratitude is the fertile soil in the garden of existence, nurturing the seeds of mindfulness. They blossom into vibrant flowers of appreciation, casting their fragrance across the landscape of our everyday experiences."

Gratitude from the Summit

"From the summit, we see the world through new eyes, appreciating the beauty that surrounds us and finding gratitude in every breathtaking moment."

Growth from Trials

"Like a phoenix rising from ashes, our truest growth emerges from the fires of life's trials, forging us into stronger, wiser beings."

Guided by Flames

"When you go down in flames, let it be a blaze that illuminates your path forward, guiding you towards a new beginning."

Hard Work and Intelligence

"Intelligence may open doors, but it's hard work that will lead you through them."

Hard Work and Success

"Hard work is the fuel that ignites intelligence's potential, transforming it into tangible success."

Helping Hand

"Extend a helping hand to those in need today so that the universe can reach out to you when you are in need."

Innocence Amidst Accusation

"Even the innocent may feel guilty in a society that constantly demands proof of one's innocence."

Inspiration from Going Down in Flames

"Sometimes, the most remarkable stories are born from those who dared to go down in flames, leaving a trail of inspiration and resilience in their wake."

Invitation of Raindrops

"Raindrops are nature's invitation to let go, surrender to the present moment, and dance with an open heart."

Journey of Exploration

"The world is vast, and your journey should be explored. Do not stay in one place for too long; seek new horizons."

Life's Strange Curriculum

"Life's strange curriculum unfolds in the classroom of opposing souls. Silence from the chatterers, tolerance from the obstinate, and kindness from the unkind - lessons inscribed on the heart with paradoxical ink, leaving an indelible mark of both gratitude and ambivalence."

Mindfulness is the Art

"Gratitude is the heart's silent music, harmonising with the rhythm of life's blessings. Mindfulness is the art of savouring each note, of orchestrating a symphony that elevates ordinary moments to soulful masterpieces."

Music's Language of the Heart

"The melodies of music are the silent conversations of the heart, a language of the spirit that transcends words, bringing solace, serenity, and understanding to the human experience."

Nature's Contributions to Happiness

"The blowing wind, the running river, the craggy mountains, the thick forest, and the clear sky all contribute to my happiness."

Nature's Secrets

"Nature's secrets are simplicity and patience."

Nurturing Connections

"In the garden of life, connections are blooming flowers, and nurturing them is the tender touch that allows beauty to flourish."

Pause for Present Beauty

"Remember to pause and take in the beauty of the present moment in your pursuit of happiness."

Power of Inner Silence

"Amidst the world's deafening noise, the silence within us speaks the loudest."

Present Moment Awareness

"The source of now reveals itself in the stillness of this moment. It is not in some faraway place or time; it is right here, inviting you to be fully present and experience the wonder of existence."

Presumption of Innocence

"Being accused does not imply guilt, and being innocent does not ensure freedom from accusation."

Renewed Strength in Rain

"Let the rain wash away your worries, as you twirl and spin in a dance of liberation and renewed strength."

Richness of Age

"Age is a testament to the richness of life's journey; it's a reminder that you've lived, learned, and still have so much more to give."

Seeking Joy

"Don't wait for joy to find you; seek it out in the simplest of moments, because it is within your power to create your happiness."

Significance of Connections

"Connections are the threads that weave the tapestry of our existence, and in their gentle care, we find the warmth that makes life's fabric whole."

Silent Epiphanies

"Life's most precious moments are often silent epiphanies that gift us with timeless insights, guiding our steps and whispering the secrets of the universe to our souls."

Silent Symphony of Thoughts

"Silence is the canvas on which the symphony of our thoughts and emotions is painted."

Smile as Manifestation of Joy

"Your smile is a direct manifestation of the joy that dances within your soul."

Source of Life in the Present

"The present moment is the source of life in all its richness and potential. Recognise that the source of now is here, and seize the opportunity to live fully in the present."

Spreading Joy

"May you always have joy in your heart and that joy spread to those around you?"

Stardust in the Cosmos

"In the vast cosmos, we are stardust woven into the fabric of the universe, forever connected to the cosmic tapestry of existence."

Sweet Symphony of Peace

"The sweet symphony of peace replaces the discordant echoes. The key to life's mysteries lies in the spirit's language, spoken through the melodic strains of music."

Symphonies of the Spirit

"Musical symphonies transcend words, becoming the eloquent language of the spirit. Their harmonies unlock life's mysteries, ushering in a tranquil peace that dispels all strife."

Thriving Connections for Happiness

"Happiness is not a solitary pursuit; it thrives in the connections we forge and the smiles we ignite in the hearts of others."

Triumph at the Peak

"At the peak, we feel a sense of triumph and accomplishment, knowing that we overcame obstacles to reach this moment of glory."

Unfettered Expression

"Let your voice soar like a bird's song, unaffected by the thoughts or opinions of others."

Unwrap Joy Each Day

"Remember, joy is not an elusive treasure; rather, it is a precious gift that we unwrap each day through acts of kindness, love, and self-care."

Verses of Love and Diversity

"Through the verses of love, we discover that diversity is the radiant spectrum of our human experience, and in connection, we find the common heartbeat that unites us all."

Weaver of Existence's Tapestry

"You are both the weaver and the thread in the tapestry of existence. Create a masterpiece that reflects the essence of your soul by unfolding your myth with intention."

Wholehearted Pursuit

"In the world of dreams and ambitions, half-heartedness leads to nowhere."

Wishes for Joy

"May you always be filled with joy, no matter what your circumstances are?"

Inspiration and Motivation

Fuelling the Soul

"To fuel the soul is to invest in the eternal. It is the heartbeat of our passions, the melody of our dreams, and the fire that keeps our spirits alive."

- Shree Shambav

Adaptation like the Wind

"The wind changes direction and intensity like life, reminding us to adapt and remain flexible."

Adversity and Resilience

"Like a dark cloud before the downpour, adversity often heralds the cleansing rain of resilience and strength."

Alive and Breathing Stars

"The stars are like the trees in the forest, alive and breathing. And they're watching me."

Amidst the chaos

"Amidst the chaos of life, the source of now is not a distant destination—it is right here, within you, waiting to be discovered and embraced."

Beauty of the Heart's Glow

"In the grand symphony of existence, the most enchanting beauty is not etched on the face but is the radiant glow that emanates from the depths of a pure and kind heart."

Belief in Overcoming Challenges

"Believe in your abilities to overcome any challenges that may arise."

Boundless Potential of Life

"Just as the wind carries the seeds of new life, life is full of boundless potential and possibilities."

Butterflies and Metamorphosis

"Butterflies dance upon the flowers, whispering tales of metamorphosis and the magic of embracing one's true self."

Calm Amid Life's Storms

"Be the calm that rises above the chaos amid life's storms, and you'll find the strength to weather any tempest that comes your way."

Compassion in Shadows

"In the shadows of desperation, a thief appears as a man in need, motivated by unseen circumstances. Compassion, not judgement, reveals the facets of his story."

Courage of Optimism

"Optimism is a way of life, not just a state of mind. It takes courage to see the good in people, to keep hope alive even in the direst of circumstances, and to believe that things will improve."

Dark Moments as Catalysts

"In the darkest moments, just before the downpour of change, there is the profound opportunity for growth and transformation."

Dreams as Soul Windows

"Dreams are windows into our souls, and a beautiful dream is the ray of light that shines through them."

Embrace Beauty with Butterflies

"In the presence of butterflies, we are reminded to embrace fleeting moments of beauty and to live life with lightness and grace."

Embrace Life's Flame

"Death's grip may loom, yet I stand unafraid, for life's flame burns within me. And when that flame fades, I shall embrace the unknown, where life and death intertwine."

Embracing Life's Impermanence

"As we reflect on the transience of life, we realise nothing lasts forever. It is this impermanence that gives meaning to every sunrise, tenderness to every goodbye, and depth to every memory. Embracing life's ephemerality permits us to embrace the present moment and etch our fleeting imprint on the canvas of time."

Enduring Beauty

"The enduring allure of beauty lies not in the features we see but in the inner illumination that transforms the ordinary into the extraordinary, casting a brilliant light from the heart."

Essence of Inner Beauty

"The true essence of beauty is not physical; rather, it is the gentle glow that emanates from within and illuminates the heart, painting the world with grace."

Essence of Nature's Thrill

"Meadows would bore without greenery, and woods would be silent without birds and insects. There would have been no thrill had the stream or brook not babbled or trickled."

Evolution of the Soul

"The cycle of life and death is an evolutionary process for the soul, where each rebirth brings greater knowledge, comprehension, and freedom."

Finding Hope in Dark Clouds

"Never fear the dark cloud before the pouring rain, for it is the prelude to nature's most profound acts of cleansing and rejuvenation."

Gift of a Beautiful Day

"A beautiful day is a gift from the heavens, a precious treasure to be savoured and cherished."

Glimmer Amid Challenges

"The light peeking through the gloomy cloud serves as a reminder that even amidst life's challenges, there is always a glimmer of possibility and beauty."

Glimmer of Light

"Remember that even the smallest glimmer of light has the power to dispel shadows in the face of the darkest moments."

Glory in Standing Up

"Having the courage to stand up for what we believe in is our greatest glory, not winning every battle."

Graceful Movement of Life

"A dancing flower sways with the rhythm of life, graceful and carefree, a symbol of the beauty in movement."

Guiding Light of Fireflies

"Fireflies, nature's living lanterns, guide us through the night, lighting our path with their mesmerising glow."

Guiding Light of Moonlight

"Moonlight reminds us that there is still light to guide us, even in the darkest of nights."

Harmony of Music

"Music is the whisper of the soul, a harmonious language that unveils the secrets of life, ushering in peace and abolishing strife."

Haven in the Woods

"The woods are a haven where the world's stresses fade away and nature's beauty takes centre stage."

Heart's Hues on the Canvas

"The hues of our hearts and the rhythm of our soul are painted on the canvas of a beautiful dream."

Hope Illuminates Darkness

"Where there is hope, there is a way forward. The light of hope can illuminate even the darkest of times and point us towards a brighter tomorrow."

Hope in Dark Times

"The flickering dance of fireflies reminds us that even in the darkest times, there is always a glimmer of hope."

Identity and Purpose

"Identity is the question, and purpose is the answer. When we delve into the depths of who we are, we discover the guiding star that illuminates our path."

Intentional Crafting of Destiny

"In the tapestry of fate, every stitch of action weaves the fabric of our destiny, urging us to craft each moment with intention and purpose."

Intricate Patterns of Destiny

"In the river of existence, every ripple of thought, every wave of words, and every current of action creates the intricate patterns of our destiny, forever bound by the unbroken chain of 'cause and effect.'"

Invitation of Sunrise

"Every sunrise is an invitation to rise and make someone's day brighter."

Journey of Discovery

"The journey of life is not about arriving at a destination, but about discovering the beauty and meaning along the way."

Journey of the Soul

"The soul's true home is a place of inconceivable truce and bliss, and life's journey is a quest to return to that state of divine union."

Legacy of Light

"A candle may melt and its fire may go out, but the light it provided will live on in the hearts of those who witnessed it."

Letting Go for New Beginnings

"Allow yourself to be carried towards new beginnings by letting go of things that no longer serve you, like leaves withering in the wind."

Metamorphosis in Nature's Ballet

"Amidst nature's ballet, a stone's burden metamorphoses into the tender clasp of a protector, offering refuge to a delicate leaf in the tumultuous winds of life's journey."

Music's Thread in Existence

"In the tapestry of existence, music is the thread that weaves emotions into the fabric of our hearts, creating a symphony of peace that resonates through the soul."

Nature's Poetry

"In Nature's cycle, we find profound poetry of existence, where birth, death, and rebirth compose the verses of life's timeless song."

Nature's Universal Language

"Nature speaks a universal language, understood by every living being in the universe. It whispers in the wind, sings in the rain, and rustles through the trees, reminding us of the interconnectedness of all life."

Nurturing Your Thoughts

"Words are like seeds; what you plant in your mind grows and shapes your reality."

Obstacles as Stepping Stones

"Obstacles are stepping stones to resilience; with each challenge we conquer, we forge the path to our strength."

Ocean of Being

"You are not merely a drop lost in the vast sea; you embody the entire ocean within the essence of your being."

Optimism's Abundance

"Optimism is the belief that the glass can be replenished and even overflowed with abundance. It is more than simply seeing the glass as half full."

Pause in Distractions

"In a world full of distractions, pause and feel the world around you - the gentle rhythm of raindrops, the laughter of children, and the pulse of humanity's collective heartbeat."

Persistence in Pursuing Dreams

"Giving up is never an option when your dreams and passions are at stake. Keep going, keep believing, and you will succeed."

Persistence of the Moon's Glow

"The moon may hide behind a dark cloud, but it never fails to shine."

Poetry in Nature's Cycle

"Nature's cycle, a poetic reflection of life's eternal dance."

Poetry of Love

"The true poetry of love resides not in the uttered words but in the tender symphony that echoes within the spaces of unspoken understanding."

Power of Words

"Words, like seeds, grow and bear fruit in your life. Choose them carefully."

Resilience of the Human Spirit

"The darkest moments are not the end, but a catalyst for new beginnings, reminding us of the resilience of the human spirit."

Restoration by the Sun

"The bright sun restores light and new life, hope, and freshness to all living things."

Rewards of Commitment

"Life rewards those who pursue their goals with unwavering commitment, not those who approach them with half-hearted intentions."

Rising After Falling

"Our greatest achievement is rising every time we fall, rather than never falling."

Savouring Each Heartbeat

"Life's fleeting nature reminds us to savour each heartbeat because even though no one lives forever, the echo of our presence lingers in the hearts we touch."

Scars and Renewal

"In the poetry of heartbreak and healing, we discover the profound truth that scars are but the footprints of our journey, and in their wake, we find the seeds of our renewal."

Silence of the Trees

"The silence of the trees is sometimes the only sound you need to hear."

Silent Wisdom of the Woods

"Deep in the woods, silence speaks louder than words."

Simplicity of Life

"Life is quite simple, but we continue to complicate it."

Source of Now Within

"Don't look outside yourself for the source of now. It dwells within the depths of your being, beckoning you to be fully present and engaged in the magic of the present moment."

Stillness in the Woods

"Deep within the woods, you can find your soul's stillness and your mind's silence."

Strength through Challenges

"Good drivers aren't born on smooth roads. Smooth seas do not produce good sailors. Clear skies do not make for good pilots. A problem-free life does not produce a strong person. Be courageous enough to face life's challenges. Rather than asking life, 'why me,' say, 'try me.'"

Symphony of Existence

"In the symphony of existence, every scent, sound, caress, sight, and flavour is a fleeting note played by Prakriti—an ephemeral melody, here in one moment, gone in the next."

Symphony of Nature's Whisper

"Only the most profound souls can hear the symphony created by the rustling of leaves and the whisper of the wind in the enigmatic setting of the woods."

The Language of Leaves

"Each leaf is a verse, each breeze a lullaby—nature does not preach, it invites. And when we listen not with ears, but with reverence, the Earth becomes scripture written in green."

Thief and Liar as Reflections

"A thief is only a reflection of unfulfilled needs within the domain of necessity, and a liar is a symphony of fear, orchestrating a delicate dance with truth."

Training the Heart

"If you train your eyes to see the good in others, you can unconsciously train your heart to love them."

True Friend as Compass

"A true friend is more than just a companion for today; they are the link to shared values and the compass guiding us to a better tomorrow."

Unspoken Love's Tapestry

"In the unspoken spaces between hearts, love weaves its most intricate tapestry, where words left unsaid echo louder than those spoken."

Unveiling True Wealth

"A beggar remains oblivious to the treasure within, unable to unveil the true wealth concealed beneath the layers of circumstance and perception."

View After the Climb

"The best view comes after the most strenuous climb."

Vision Amid Chaos

"Amid chaos and confusion, a beautiful vision can provide us with the serenity that brings us peace."

Whisper of the Soul

"A beautiful dream is the whisper of your soul, reminding you of the magic that resides within."

Wholehearted Efforts

"Half-hearted efforts yield half-hearted results; only those who give it their all can truly taste success."

Wisdom of Trees

"The trees speak to me, reminding me of my roots and my reach."

Dreams and Aspirations

Dreams and Aspirations

"Passions are the stars that guide us through life's boundless darkness, illuminating our path with the light of purpose and fulfilment."

- *Shree Shambav*

Achieve greatness

"Never accept a life less than what you can live. Push yourself to your limits and you will achieve greatness."

Aligning with the Universe

"Make a wish on a shooting star; the universe will align to hear your heart's desires."

Appreciating Endings

"The end of the road can be a beautiful place if you take the time to look around and appreciate the journey."

Architects of Aspiration

"Aspiration is the silent architect, drawing the blueprint of our dreams on the canvas of reality. Dreams compose the melody in the symphony of existence, while aspiration conducts the orchestra, harmonising our journey to the crescendo of fulfilment."

Ardour of Dreams

"The world has no room for half-hearted dreams; it craves the ardour of those who dare to dream big and act with full conviction".

Aspirations' Depths

"To fathom the depths of a person's essence, one must delve into the uncharted waters of their aspirations, for there, amidst the dreams and desires, lies the true compass of their heart and mind."

Battlefield of Dreams

"On the dream battlefield, doubt is the silent assassin. Stand firm in your convictions and watch as the influence of doubt fades."

Belief in Self

"You can achieve greatness if you have big dreams and believe in yourself."

Best teacher

"Life itself is the best teacher. It instils in us the virtues of endurance, tenacity, and the determination to pursue our goals regardless of the circumstances."

Bright Guidance

"Although the moon appears alone in the sky, it shines brightly enough to light up the darkest of nights and guide us on our way."

Character's Depth

"The true measure of a person's character lies not in their past accomplishments, but in the lofty aspirations that ignite their soul, for it is in those aspirations that we find the map to their heart and mind."

Choosing Happiness

"People who are dissatisfied focus on their flaws. People who are content focus on their possessions. Choose to be happy rather than unhappy."

Choosing Positivity

"People with a negative outlook on life are miserable. Instead of being unhappy, decide to see the wonder and beauty in the world."

Confronting Fears

"If you want to be successful, you must confront your fears. Success is on the other side of fear."

Conquering Doubt

"Doubt is the thief of dreams; slay it with unwavering self-belief, and watch your aspirations flourish."

Conspiring Universe

"When you work for a good cause, the universe conspires to help you achieve it."

Cosmic Revelations

"The universe reveals its secrets in the verses of cosmic poetry, and we become the scribes of its majesty. With words as our guide, we embark on a journey through the cosmos, where the boundless and the infinitesimal dance in lyrical harmony."

Creative Palette

"Imagination is an artist's palette, and inspiration is the brush that paints the vivid tapestry of creativity."

Dance of Existence

"In the dance of existence, shake off the weight of emptiness, and twirl with the rhythm of your own heartbeat, filling every step with the richness of your soul."

Doubt's Door

"Doubt may knock on your dream door, but only you have the key to lock it and pave the way to success."

Dreams as Blueprints

"A beautiful dream is more than a fantasy; it is the blueprint for our future."

Dreams' Significance

"Dreams take centre stage in the heart's theatre, donning the costumes of desire and performing the ballet of aspiration. They dance together, creating the grand spectacle of a life filled with purpose and passion."

Embracing Challenges

"Never take the easy way out; always choose the less-travelled path to discover new opportunities."

Embracing Change

"The wind teaches us that nothing remains constant in life, and we must learn to embrace change."

Facing Doubt

"When doubt whispers in your ear, roar with confidence and see how dreams can thrive in the face of uncertainty."

Finding Contentment

"We find the warmth of contentment in the embrace of life's little pleasures, like a cosy blanket on a chilly day, wrapping us in simple joy."

Fleeting Moments

"In the blink of an eye, a shooting star leaves a trail, reminding us of the fleeting nature of time and the importance of savouring the moment."

Fuelling the Soul

"To fuel the soul is to invest in the eternal. It is the heartbeat of our passions, the melody of our dreams, and the fire that keeps our spirits alive."

Harnessing Life's Winds

"Life, like the wind, can be unpredictable, but we can learn to harness its strength and move forward with grace."

Hope in Darkness

"The light peeping through the gloomy clouds reminds us that even in our darkest moments, hope persists, waiting to illuminate our path."

Identity and Purpose

"Our identity is the canvas, and our purpose is the masterpiece we paint on it, evolving with each stroke of self-discovery."

Imagery and Inspiration

"Within the labyrinth of the mind, imagery is the map, and inspiration is the compass, guiding us through the intricate passages of our imagination."

Impact of Action

"Never underestimate your ability to affect change in the world. Every step you take in that direction inspires others to act on their beliefs."

Inner Strength

"Just as the sun's rays pierce through gloomy clouds, our inner strength can shine through adversity, casting a light on the way forward."

Inspiration's Light

"In the realm of imagery, inspiration is the sun, casting light upon the canvas of the mind, giving birth to landscapes of possibility."

Intensity of Purpose

"When passion and understanding fuse with your work, distractions fade away, consumed by the intensity of purpose and commitment."

Journey of Life

"Life is a journey, and the lessons we learn along the way help us become who we are."

Joy in the Present

"Joy resides in the tender moments we grasp in the present, like fireflies on a summer's night, lighting up the darkness of our memories."

Key to Creativity

"Fairy tales are the key to unlocking the creativity that exists within us."

Learning from Mistakes

"Mistakes illuminate our path, guiding us towards a brighter future filled with knowledge and self-awareness, like stars in the night sky."

Life's Lessons

"Life is a series of lessons, some more difficult than others, but all crucial in shaping who we are."

Luminescent Trails

"Fireflies, like stars in motion, weave their luminescent trails through the night, leaving traces of enchantment wherever they go."

Moon's Silent Hope

"The moon may appear alone in the night sky, but it is never truly alone, because it always carries the hopes and dreams of those who gaze upon it."

New Beginnings

"Every ending is a new beginning, and every path leads to a different destination."

Optimistic Dreams

"A beautiful dream is the fragrance of optimism that fills our souls and the beacon of light that guides us through the darkest of times."

Overcoming Fear

"Fear impedes progress. Don't let it get in your way. Face your fears and begin moving towards your goals."

Peace Is Not Found, But Built

"Peace is not stumbled upon; it's crafted from forgiveness, acceptance, and the gentle refusal to carry what isn't yours."

Persistence in Pursuit

"Any dream can come true if we dare to pursue it with zeal and persistence."

Power of Words and Actions

"Your words and actions have the potential to change the world. Never underestimate the power of your voice to affect positive change."

Power of the Mind

"The Mind controls all receptors; it is powerful, the strongest."

Prioritise Yourself

"Never accept someone who sees you as an option. You deserve to be treated as a priority."

Purpose in Work

"It's not the amount of work that breaks you; it's the lack of purpose and passion that makes the load unbearable. Find meaning, and even the most arduous task can become a stepping stone to greatness."

Pursuing Dreams

"To make your dreams a reality, act on them. Dream big, but work even harder to make your dreams come true."

Rejecting Limiting Mindsets

"Never accept a mindset that restricts your potential. Have faith in yourself and your abilities to accomplish great things."

Reminder of Magic

"A shooting star can serve as a gentle reminder that magic is all around us, just waiting to be discovered."

Rising Above Challenges

"The storm may rage, but the indomitable human spirit has the power to rise above, illuminating the darkest skies with the brilliance of hope and courage."

Rising Above Doubt

"Like a majestic eagle soaring above the thunderclouds, rise above the storm of doubt and fear, and let your vision guide you to new heights of greatness."

Seeds of Dreams

"Dreams are the seeds of our future, and a beautiful dream is the garden in which they grow."

Stardust Trails

"As they dance across the night, shooting stars leave trails of stardust as a reminder that dreams can come true."

Stars of Hope

"Dreams are like stars; they may appear distant, but they shine brightest when the night is darkest."

Striving for Greatness

"Never settle for mediocrity; always strive for greatness and follow your dreams to success."

Symphony of Aspirations

"In the grand symphony of a person's life, the notes of their past may provide a melody, but it's the harmonious chords of their aspirations that reveal the depth and richness of their soul."

The Invisible Currency

"Time is the only wealth we never see until it's gone. Spend it not in haste, but in meaning."

True Love's Worth

"Never accept a love that does not make you feel alive. True love is worth the wait and the fight."

Universe's Poetry

"The universe is the canvas, and poetry is the brush that paints the mysteries of the universe. With each verse, we explore the boundless cosmos, discovering the constellations of our imagination."

Unlimited Dreams

"Never limit your dreams. Instead, dream big and let your ambitions soar."

Venturing Into the Unknown

"Never settle for a haven; instead, venture into the unknown. The journey will be worthwhile."

Vision of the Future

"A beautiful dream is a glimpse of the future that we can create, not just a figment of our imagination."

Whispers of the Wind

"The wind is a constant reminder that everything is interconnected and that we are all part of a larger, more intricate web of existence."

Work for a Cause

"Work for a cause, not for applause. Live your life to express yourself, not to impress others."

Lessons from Adversity

Turning Challenges into Growth

"Like a phoenix rising from the ashes, our truest growth emerges from the fires of life's trials, forging us into stronger, wiser beings."

- Shree Shambav

Achieve Great Things

"When you pursue your passions and put your heart and soul into your endeavours, you can achieve great things. Believe in yourself and never hold back. Life is short, so make the most of it by giving it your all."

Action Turns Dreams into Reality

"Unless you do, your dreams will remain just that - dreams. Take action and make your dreams a reality. No one else can do it for you, and nothing will change unless you take the first step. So go ahead, take a chance, and do what you can to turn your dreams into a tangible reality."

Aim for the Stars

"Aim high. Set your goals high and let your imagination run wild. Allow your aspirations to soar by believing in the impossibility. Aim for the stars and watch your world change because the size of your dreams determines the extent of your success."

Anchor of Hope

"Hope is the soul's anchor; cling to it tightly because it will help you get through life's storms."

Beautiful Places

"Sometimes the hardest paths lead us to the most beautiful places."

Boundless Potential

"You are capable of great things and have boundless potential. Break free from the chains holding you back by having faith in yourself. Explore new possibilities and embrace new challenges, and you will find success beyond your wildest dreams."

Calm Amidst Tempest

"The tempest of life may toss us around, but within us lies the calm that can weather any storm."

LIFE CHANGING JOURNEY

Character from Difficulty

"Difficult paths breed character and resilience, which is what makes us strong."

Company in Solitude

"The moon may appear alone in the night sky, but it is always accompanied by the stars that twinkle beside it, reminding us that there is always the company of light even in solitude."

Confronting Fear for Success

"If you want to be successful, you must confront your fears. Success is on the other side of fear."

Conspiring Universe

"The universe will conspire to make your dreams a reality if you dare to pursue them."

Dance with the Rain

"When faced with hardship, don't seek shelter; step outside and dance with the rain as your partner."

Daring Pursuits

"When you dare to pursue your dreams, they become a reality. Take a risk and follow your passions, no matter what obstacles stand in your way."

Desire for Abundance

"In the pursuit of abundance, the desire for more can make even the many seem like too few."

Echoes of Karma

"Karma is the echoed reflection of our thoughts, words, and actions, echoing through time and space to shape our present and future realities."

Embrace Life Fully

"Life is short, but it is broad enough for those who fully embrace it."

Embrace of Nature's Light

"When you are deeply enveloped in darkness, throwing yourself into nature's arms will reveal a new ray of hope."

Embracing Light and Shadow

"Where the light shines, shadows follow. Embrace both the bright and dark moments in life, as they each play a role in shaping who you are. Learn from your experiences and use them to grow, both in the light and in the shadow."

Emergence in Desperation

"In the shadowed corners of desperation, a thief emerges, not born of malice but of unmet needs seeking the light of survival."

Endurance and Reward

"The best parts of life often await us at the end of arduous journeys."

Equality of Birth

"Some people are born with more advantages than others; they are not born better than others."

Fear as a Guidepost

"Fear is not your adversary; rather, it serves as a guidepost pointing you towards the challenges you must face and overcome in your quest for growth."

Fearlessness and Courage

"Being fearless does not imply being courageous. It implies that you continue despite your fear."

Fear's Impediment

"Fear impedes progress. Don't let it get in your way. Face your fears and begin moving toward your goals."

Finding Light in Darkness

"Rainbows are a natural reminder that there is always light and beauty to be found, even amidst the darkest storm."

Follow Your Heart

"Go with all your heart. When you follow your passions and pursue your dreams with every ounce of your being, you will find true success and fulfilment. Don't hold back, give it your all, and watch as the universe conspires to make your wildest dreams come true."

Forging Souls

"Souls are forged in the furnaces of adversity. Each wound is a testament to inner strength; each scar is a story of unyielding resilience."

Gaze at the Stars

"Keep your gaze fixed on the stars and your feet firmly planted on the ground. Maintain your focus on your goals while remaining aware of your surroundings. Keep your dreams in mind and work hard to make them a reality, but be grateful for the journey and lessons learned along the way."

Go the Extra Mile

"Go the extra mile. It's the little extra effort that makes all the difference in life. Whether it's in your personal or professional life, putting in that extra effort separates the average from the exceptional. So go above and beyond, and watch as opportunities and success come your way."

Growth Through Struggle

"Struggle is not something to be afraid of; rather, it is an opportunity to grow stronger and wiser in the face of adversity."

Hope's Strength

"Hope is the anchor of the soul; keep it strong, and it will keep you steady."

Human Actions

"The inequalities that exist in our world result from human actions and decisions, not some cosmic injustice."

Inner Purity

"Outer success is merely an illusion without inner purity."

Invest in Your Dreams

"Invest in your dreams. Your aspirations are the seed that can grow into a fulfilling and meaningful life. Nurture them with hard work, dedication, and a strong belief in yourself. The time and effort you put into your dreams today will pay off in the form of a bright future tomorrow."

Learning from Time

"Yesterday was a lesson, today is an opportunity, and tomorrow is an unknown."

Lessons from Mountains

"The mountains may appear intimidating and insurmountable, but each step we take towards them teaches us more about our strength and fortitude."

Letting Go and Renewal

"Let go of the past, wash away your pain, anger, and hatred, and emerge refreshed, renewed, and pure like the waterfall."

Life's Boomerang

"Life is a boomerang. What you give, you get."

Life's Duality

"Just as the wind can be both gentle and fierce, life can be both beautiful and challenging."

Lonely Echo

"One who adamantly shuts out others' perspectives often discovers a lonely echo for his own views."

Making the Best of Circumstances

"We are all born with unique talents, abilities, and circumstances, and it is up to us to make the best of what we have."

Metaphysics and Navigation

"Ignoring the existence of metaphysics is like attempting to navigate a ship without a compass; it may appear possible at first, but it ultimately leads to a meaningless and unfulfilling journey."

Mistakes as Stepping Stones

"Do not be afraid of making mistakes. They are not failures; rather, they are stepping stones to success."

Mountains of Resilience

"The mountains serve as a reminder that, even in the face of seemingly insurmountable obstacles, we are capable of achieving great heights, demonstrating both the resilience of the human spirit and the strength of the earth."

Navigating Life's Storms

"Life, like a raging storm, can be both destructive and transformative. It is up to us to navigate the storm and emerge stronger, wiser, and more resilient on the other side."

Necessity and Invention

"Necessity is the mother of invention; when confronted with a problem, it drives us to seek new and innovative solutions."

Occult Knowledge

"Occult knowledge is not meant for the curious or the faint-hearted, but for the seekers who are ready to unlock the mysteries of the universe and discover the true nature of existence."

Perseverance Yields Results

"The only way to fail is to stop trying. Continue to move forward and expand as you see how your perseverance yields amazing results."

Persistence in Pursuit

"Never give up on a dream. Keep pushing forward, even when the journey is tough. Your dreams are worth fighting for, and the persistence and resilience you develop along the way will only make you stronger. Keep believing, keep striving, and never give up on what truly matters to you."

Potential for Positive Difference

"We may not be born equal, but we can all make a positive difference in the world."

Power of Lateral Thinking

"Lateral thinking is a powerful tool for overcoming obstacles and generating new ideas."

Power of Starting Over

"Starting over is a powerful act of self-recreation, not a setback. The canvas of your life is ready for the brushstrokes of tenacity and the colours of endless possibilities."

Pushing Beyond Limits

"Challenge your limits and break free from your comfort zone. Growth and progress come from stepping outside of what's familiar and facing new obstacles. Embrace change, take risks, and never stop learning. The greatest achievements come from pushing beyond what you thought was possible."

Pushing Boundaries

"Don't be afraid to step out of your comfort zone and test the boundaries of what you believe is possible. Embrace new experiences and take on new challenges, and you will find that you are capable of far more than you ever imagined."

Realm of Self-Affirmation

"In the realm of self-affirmation, declaring 'I can' and boasting 'I am unrivalled' may seem empowering, yet it binds the individual to the realm of consequences, for as long as 'I' remains the doer."

Refinement Through Tough Times

"Tough times in life are not meant to define you, but to refine and strengthen you."

Reservoir of Strength

"A reservoir of strength exists deep within me, waiting to be tapped when life's challenges arise."

Resilience in Adversity

"When faced with adversity, let resilience be your armour and tenacity be your fuel. Never give up on the things that matter to you."

Resourceful Creativity

"Lateral thinking is about more than just being smart; it's about being resourceful and creative."

Shadows of Success

"Success always comes with shadows. The greater your achievements, the greater the obstacles you will face. But don't be afraid of the shadows, for they are simply a testament to the light you bring to the world. Keep pushing forward and let your success continue to shine."

Shine Bright

"Let your light shine bright. Glitter and sparkle all day with positive energy and good vibes. Be the shining star that brings joy and happiness to those around you. Remember, you were born to stand out and make a difference in the world."

Silent Work, Loud Success

"Work in silence and let your success make the noise. Let your actions and results speak for themselves. Focus on your goals and put in the effort, without worrying about recognition or validation. True success is not about the applause you receive, but about the satisfaction you feel from achieving your dreams."

Solitude for Self-Reflection

"Solitude is the choice to be alone for self-reflection and happiness."

Solitude's Brilliance

"The moon may appear to be alone in the sky, but it serves as a constant reminder that even in solitude, one can still shine brightly and dispel darkness."

Start Where You Are

"Do what you can, with what you have, where you are. You don't need to have everything figured out or have all the resources you need to start pursuing your goals. Just start with what you have, and you will find that you can accomplish more than you ever imagined."

Staying Grounded

"The wind reminds us to stay grounded and rooted, even as we allow ourselves to be carried forward by the flow of life."

Stepping Stones to Greatness

"The road to success is paved with obstacles, but they are stepping stones to greatness."

Strength in Lateral Thinking

"Lateral thinking is like a muscle; the more you work it, the stronger it gets."

Strength in Setbacks

"When faced with adversity, remember that setbacks are only temporary. You have the strength to persevere. 'Keep going.'"

Strength of Mind

"A strong mind is resilient and can easily overcome difficulties."

The Realm of 'Not Mine'

"The essence of 'Me' encompasses the mind and body, while 'Mine' extends to possessions, knowledge, and relationships. Everything beyond this, beyond our control, falls into the realm of 'Not Mine.'"

Thread of Compassion

"Amidst the intricate web of life's challenges, the thread of compassion weaves a tapestry of boundless understanding and enduring strength."

Time and Dreams

"Never give up on a dream just because of the time it will take to accomplish it. The time will pass anyway. Keep your eyes on the prize and persevere through the challenges, knowing that your persistence will pay off in the end. Your dream is worth the journey, so keep pushing forward and never give up."

Transforming Pain

"No one can take your pain away from you, but you can choose how you carry it and transform it into strength."

Turning Pain into Wisdom

"Turn your pain into wisdom. Take the lessons from your struggles and use them to gain a deeper understanding of yourself and the world around you. Turn your challenges into a source of strength and growth."

Turning Sorrow into Joy

"Use the experiences that once brought you sorrow to create joy and positivity in your life. Allow every adversity to serve as a stepping stone to a brighter future."

Unleash Your Potential

"Don't limit yourself. Break free from societal constraints and your own beliefs. When you unleash your full potential and dare to explore new possibilities, the sky is the limit. Dream big, shoot for the stars, and let no one or anything hold you back."

Wonderful Destinations

"Difficult paths often lead to wonderful destinations, but they demand tenacity and determination."

The Power of Kindness

Spreading Compassion and Love

"To spread love and compassion is to light a candle in the heart, and by the warm glow of that candle, we can illuminate the deepest recesses of humanity."

- Shree Shambav

Anchored in Kindness

"Adversity may sweep us away, but our unwavering acts of kindness are the anchors that keep us grounded, reminding us that even in the roughest seas, we can find our way back to hope."

Aspiration Towards Illumination

"Love of humanity! Love of God! Love of Truth! Aspiration towards the illumination of the mind is the utterly perfect element and way of life."

Balancing Power

"Balancing the scales of empathy, compassion, and mercy with the foundation of peace and order is the solemn duty of those who hold power, for in harmony, true strength is found."

Be the Light

"A single act of kindness has the power to brighten someone's day and leave a lasting impression. 'Be the light in someone's life.'"

Bridging Love and Non-Violence

"Let love and kindness be the flowing river, while mastery of the mind, thought, and word becomes the bridge to non-violence, greening the desolate areas of our planet."

Bringing Sunshine

"Even the smallest acts of kindness can brighten someone's day, so be the ray of sunshine that radiates warmth and compassion."

Celestial Music

"Beyond the bounds of our mortal world, celestial music echoes throughout the celestial spheres, inviting us to glimpse the celestial realm and embrace the sublime wonders of the cosmos."

Celestial Nocturne

"In the night sky, celestial music orchestrates a mesmerising nocturne, inviting us to lose ourselves in its transcendent rhythm and find solace in the grandeur of the universe."

Choose Kindness

"Choose kindness and let compassion be your guide in a world where anything is possible."

Choosing Peace

"When anger prowls at the door of your heart, remember that it is a hungry beast that devours reason and compassion. Choose the path of peace, and let compassion be your candle, illuminating even the darkest parts of your existence."

Consequences of Self-Affirmation

"In the realm of self-affirmation, declaring 'I can' and boasting 'I am unrivalled' may seem empowering, yet it binds the individual to the realm of consequences, for as long as 'I' remains the doer."

Creating Ripple Effects

"Choose to be the person who brings sunshine into the lives of others, because you will create a ripple effect of love and happiness."

Creating Waves of Kindness

"Compassion and love are ripples we cast upon the world's waters, and in their gentle touch, we create waves of kindness that can reach even the farthest shores."

Cultivating Serenity

"Cultivating inner peace is like tending to a soul garden; with each mindful breath, we nurture the blossoms of serenity that flourish within."

Deeds Define

"A tree can be remembered by its fruits and blooms, whereas a man can be identified only by his actions. A good deed is never forgotten, but a wicked act will always revert to haunt you."

Depths of Character

"True glory is found in the depths of our character, the kindness we exhibit, and the impact we have on the lives of others."

Desire for Abundance

"In the pursuit of abundance, the desire for more can make even the many seem like too few."

Discovering Passion

"In the pursuit of our passions, we discover the symphony of our souls, with each note a reminder of the beauty that resides within us."

Embrace Nature

"It is my nature to save him, just as the scorpion's nature is to sting. Why should I forsake the essence of my nature, just as the scorpion does not abandon his?"

Empathy and Kindness

"Empathy is all about realising echoes of other people in yourself. Whereas kindness begins with comprehending the suffering and grief around you, a wonderful gesture can reach a wound that can be relieved by compassion."

Enduring Legacy

"In the tapestry of life, each thread weaves its own story, and while no one lives forever, the legacy of our moments endures."

Expanding Love

"Expand and increase your love to where rage cannot touch it."

Father's Love

"Father's love, like invisible air, breathes life into our being, providing the oxygen we need for growth and our journey through life."

Gathering Pearls of Purpose

"Embrace the plunge with heart and soul, for it's in the depths that you gather pearls of passion and purpose."

Goal of Life

"The goal of life is to make everyone and everything around you happy, with your acts of kindness and compassion."

Guardian's Embrace

"In the dance of elements, a stone's weight becomes a guardian's embrace, sheltering a delicate leaf from the tumultuous winds of life."

Guidance of Kindness

"Choosing kindness is an act of grace; if kindness eludes you, let the simple principle guide you: do no harm to the beings who share this existence."

Guiding Lights of Compassion

"Even when we are mired in despair, unwavering acts of compassion are the lights that guide us back to the surface of hope."

Guiding Lights of Empathy

"Let empathy guide your understanding, compassion soothe your heart, and forgiveness light the way to a brighter world in the pursuit of peace and order."

Happiness Multiplies

"The key to finding happiness is to make others happy. Your happiness multiplies when you uplift and inspire those around you."

Healing Touch of Kindness

"Kindness is a gentle touch that heals unseen wounds, whereas compassion is empathy that binds us together in our common human experience."

Holiness and Hatred

"Do you believe divinity will remain in you while your heart is bitter? Because hatred and holiness cannot coexist in one's heart."

Humanity's Tapestry

"In the tapestry of humanity, compassion is the thread that weaves us together, and understanding is the pattern that celebrates our differences."

Inner Radiance

"Beauty is the light that shines from within, not just what you can see on the outside."

Invaluable Lessons

"Even the tiniest creatures have the power to deepen your faith and broaden your horizons. A seed that sprouts from the ground can teach you something invaluable. Not only does his work offer us wisdom but also love, passion, hope, and patience. He is flawless, and everything he creates reflects that."

Journey of Love

"In just a moment, a heart flutters. In an hour, fondness blooms. In a day, love whispers its name. But in a lifetime, memories etch deeply."

Kindness Ripples

"An act of kindness is a ripple that can create a wave of hope, touching the lives of countless others."

Kindness in Adversity

"In life's storms of adversity, kindness is the lighthouse that guides us through the darkest of nights, showing us that hope can be found even when all seems lost."

Law of Reciprocity

"Life is a boomerang. What you give, you get."

Lighting Candles of Love

"To spread love and compassion is to light a candle in the heart, and by the warm glow of that candle, we can illuminate the deepest recesses of humanity."

Link Between Happiness

"Your happiness is inextricably linked to the happiness you bring to others. Accept the power of kindness and compassion to live a happy life."

LIFE CHANGING JOURNEY

Living the Ultimate Truth

"When you are compassionate towards others who are in need, in pain and suffering, in misery and grief, and seek to ease them, you are living the ultimate truth."

Loneliness of Closed Minds

"One who adamantly shuts out others' perspectives often discovers a lonely echo for his own views."

Love's Captivating Enigma

"Love is a captivating enigma, a symphony of emotions in which each note is a mystery waiting to be solved."

Measure of Love

"Time measures love in moments, but forgetting is a chapter that never closes."

Mercy and Compassion

"Mercy and compassion are the keystones of a just society, but they must stand side by side with the pillars of order and peace, for together, they build a stronger world."

Mystery of Love

"In the dance of hearts, love weaves its mystery, casting an enchanting spell that leaves us forever intrigued."

Nature's Harmony

"When considering coexistence, two words spring to mind: coexistence and harmony. Nature is full of life and energy, and everything is in balance there. All sentient beings, except for humans, coexist in harmony. We, humans, wreak havoc on the habitat, which will lead to disaster, eventually."

Navigating Life

"Life, like the wind, is an uncontrollable force, but we can learn to navigate it with grace and ease."

Navigating Life's Currents

"Amid life's currents, remember to take it easy—a gentle breeze navigates the path more gracefully than a tempestuous storm."

Not how they look

"What truly makes a person beautiful is how they make others feel, not how they look."

Nurturing Love and Kindness

"To master one's mind, thoughts, and words in the pursuit of non-violence is to nurture the river of love and kindness that can turn the driest hearts into green pastures."

Painting Your Life

"You hold the brush; use it to paint the picture of your life that best captures the radiance of your soul."

Possibility of Wonder

"Every day holds the possibility of doing something wonderful that lifts others and brings joy to your own heart."

Power of Kindness

"A single act of kindness has the potential to start a chain reaction that spreads love and compassion further than we can imagine."

Power of Small Acts

"Do not underestimate the power of small acts of kindness and love; they have the potential to change the lives of those around you."

Protection in Unlikely Sources

"Against the howling winds of challenge, a simple stone becomes a shield, reminding us that protection often comes from the unlikeliest of sources."

Pushing Limits

"You'll never know what you're truly capable of unless you push yourself to your limits."

Realms of 'Me' and 'Mine'

"The essence of 'Me' encompasses the mind and body, while 'Mine' extends to possessions, knowledge, and relationships. Everything beyond this, beyond our control, falls into the realm of 'Not Mine.'"

Renewing Love

"Like a clear spring, a mother's love renews our spirit and fills our hearts with a sense of renewal."

Riches of Nature's Symphony

"Amidst the chorus of nature's symphony, we learn that the richest treasures lie not in chasing illusions, but in embracing the beauty of what surrounds us."

River of Love and Kindness

"Love and kindness, a river on the arid plains of life, transforming desolation into a lush pasture of compassion."

Shrouded Knowledge

"Just like a fire covered by smoke, a mirror masked by dust. Similarly, one's knowledge gets shrouded by deep bitterness."

Smokescreen of Words

"Words can be a smokescreen, obscuring the truth behind cleverly crafted pretexts."

Soul's Currency

"Compassion and love are the most valuable commodities in the soul's currency. The more we spend, the better our lives grow, and the riches we share with others know no boundaries."

Spreading Happiness

"To experience lasting happiness, be a beacon of light for others. Making others happy will shed light on your path."

Steadfast Presence

"Amidst the tempest's fury, a steadfast stone cradles a fragile leaf, teaching us that even in the face of adversity, a guardian presence can shield and empower."

Strength in Bonds

"When we're buried in despair, the bonds we forge with others become the lifelines that pull us back to the surface, proving that even in our most challenging moments, the strength of our connections can prevail."

Strength in Unity

"Nature's wisdom unfolds as a resolute stone stands guard over a vulnerable leaf, revealing the strength of unity amidst life's storms."

Sublime Wonders

"The world is illuminated by beauty, which can be found in the most basic things."

Sunshine of Kindness

"A kind word, a smile, or a helping hand can be the sunshine that brings light and hope into someone's darkest moments."

Tapestry of Compassion

"Amidst the intricate web of life's challenges, the thread of compassion weaves a tapestry of boundless understanding and enduring strength."

The Mother We Forgot

"We sought the stars while trampling the soil that bore us—yet every breath we take is her gift, every bloom a memory of her unconditional love we so often mistake for silence."

Threads of Kindness

"In the tapestry of life, kindness and compassion are the threads that weave a beautiful and harmonious existence for all."

True Beauty

"Good character shines brighter than the most exquisite dress, for true beauty radiates from within."

Uniting Force

"Compassion is the force that unites humanity, and kindness is the language that transcends barriers."

Unveiling Love's Mystery

"Like a buried treasure, each discovery we make into the depths of love reveals a new layer of its wonderful mystery."

Uplifting Others

"The true measure of our greatness is not our achievements, but how we uplift and inspire others along the way."

Warmth

"The warmth that emanates from a kind and compassionate heart is true beauty."

LIFE CHANGING JOURNEY

Women's Empowerment

"Women emerge from the embers of adversity as flames of transformation, forged by experience and fuelled by an unwavering commitment to growth and empowerment."

Wisdom from the Ages

Timeless Insights for Life

"Life's most precious moments are often silent epiphanies that gift us with timeless insights, guiding our steps and whispering the secrets of the universe to our souls."

- Shree Shambav

Accepting Challenges

"The path to success is fraught with perils. Accept challenges, learn from them, and always keep your goals in mind."

Ageless Aspirations

"Don't let your age limit your aspirations; remember, you are never too old to learn, grow, and achieve greatness."

Ageless Pursuits

"Age is just a number; it's never too late to pursue your passions, follow your dreams, and create a life that brings you joy."

Ageless Pursuits

"You are never too old to set a new goal, dream a new dream, and embark on a new adventure."

Beautiful Destinations

"The hardest journey often leads to the most beautiful destinations."

Beware of Deception

"Don't believe everything you hear, because words can be deceiving and lies can be appealing. Only believe what you know to be true, and let your actions speak louder than any rumour or hearsay."

Beyond the Point of Giving Up

"Success is often just beyond the point at which others give up. Continue to push forward, and you'll reach heights you never imagined possible."

Bringers of Sunshine

"Those who bring sunshine into the lives of others have discovered the secret to genuine happiness and fulfilment."

Bringing Sunshine

"In a world hungry for kindness and compassion, be the one who brings sunshine into the lives of others and watch as your light shines even brighter."

Broadening Horizons

"At the top of the world, we discover a perspective that broadens our horizons and serves as a constant reminder of the infinite possibilities that lie ahead."

Brushstrokes of Emotion

"Let positive words be the brushstrokes of your emotions, painting your world in the vibrant hues of optimism and hope."

Burden of Lovelessness

"Life, devoid of the sweet nectar of love, becomes a burden too heavy to bear."

Butterfly's Reminder

"In the flutter of a butterfly's wings, we find a gentle reminder to appreciate the small moments in life and to find joy in life's simple pleasures."

Concentration's Power

"We can't think of two things at once; concentrate on the present, and the future will fall into place."

Constant Joy

"Let joy be your constant companion, and you'll discover that even in the darkest of moments, a glimmer of light shines within, guiding you towards serenity."

Crushed by Pride

"The burden of pride crushes the spirit and dulls the senses."

Cultivating Contentment

"The key to long-term happiness is to cultivate contentment and gratitude for the present moment."

Cultivating Peace

"Rash actions often breed regret, while patience and empathy cultivate a garden of peace and lasting happiness."

Daring to Soar

"On top of the world, we realise our dreams are not confined to the ground below, but can soar to great heights when we dare to chase them."

Deception of Pride

"Pride is a deceptive emotion that causes people to overestimate their abilities."

Destiny's Reflection

"As your action is, so is your destiny."

Discerning Truth

"Don't let what you hear shape your beliefs, because the noise of falsehoods frequently drowns the truth out."

Echoes of Fear

"The echoes of falsehood are the whispers of a fearful heart. In essence, a liar is a soul seeking refuge from the storms of truth."

Embrace Change's Power

"When the winds of change blow, some build walls, while others build windmills. Embrace the winds of change, harness its power, and allow it to propel you towards your dreams."

Embrace the Storms

"Embrace the storms within, for it is in the depths of struggle that the seeds of resilience and wisdom take root, blossoming into the flowers of a richer soul."

Embracing Eternal Existence

"In life, I embrace the inevitability of death, knowing that while I am alive, death cannot claim me. And when death finally arrives, I shall transcend into eternal existence."

Emptiness Breeds Freshness

"Just like a cup brimming with old tea cannot hold the fresh brew, an open heart can only be filled with new experiences when we empty our emotional cup."

Essence of True Religion

"True religion is empathy, compassion, love, and kindness. We must have faith in this religion."

Eternal Essence

"Though the physical appearance changes, the soul remains constant. In this way, everything changes around us, but nothing ever changes. The essence was always the same."

Eternal Transformation

"Like the eternal cycle of water, from rain to river to stream, religions offer a continuous journey of growth, renewal, and spiritual transformation."

Extraordinary Mundanity

"If you have joy in your heart, even the most mundane moments will become extraordinary."

Forging Fires

"Life's inherent struggles are the forging fires that shape us, mould our character, and enable us to emerge as stronger, wiser, and more compassionate beings."

Garden of Life

"Different religions are like a vibrant garden, with each blossom adding its unique colour and fragrance, enriching the world with diversity and grace."

Grace in Scars

"Meeting your scars with grace transforms pain from a prison into a path toward peace."

Gratitude Amid Chaos

"Pause and remind yourself to be grateful for the present moment, even if life is chaotic and hectic."

Guiding Compass of the Heart

"Don't lose your heart when things are uncertain; instead, let it be the compass that guides you back to your truest self."

Guiding Stars

"Passions are the stars that guide us through life's boundless darkness, illuminating our path with the light of purpose and fulfilment."

Harmonious Words

"In the symphony of life, the harmonious notes of positive words orchestrate a melody that resonates with your heart, filling your soul with joy and inspiration."

Healing Is Homecoming

"To heal is to come home to yourself, embracing every part with kindness and trust."

Hidden Depths

"Just as the moon bears its hidden face, we too harbour unseen depths within us."

Illuminate from Within

"When it's inside, don't search in the dark outside."

Illusion of Relationship

"We are born alone, live alone, and die alone. We create the illusion of relationship, love, and friendship during the intermittent. A Maya who makes us feel like we're not alone."

Inevitable Journey

"In the vast tapestry of life, the inevitable truth remains: from the low to the mighty, from the poor to the wealthy, from the weak to the powerful, and from the wicked to the virtuous, every soul must embark on the journey of departure."

Inner Power

"The truest source of power lies within, where the mind and spirit work in unison to create a force capable of overcoming any obstacle."

Intelligence and Hard Work

"Intelligence builds its achievements on the bedrock of hard work; they are a potent tandem that fuels greatness."

Joyful Navigation

"With joy as your compass, you'll navigate life's twists and turns, transforming hurdles into opportunities and spreading positivity wherever you go."

Key of Gratitude

"Gratitude is the key to understanding the true worth of what life has to offer. Accept each experience as a gift and observe how it changes your perspective."

Key to Compassion

"True compassion arises when understanding becomes the key that unlocks the door to empathy, allowing us to walk in another's shoes and truly share their journey."

Language of Compassion

"Compassion is the language of the heart, and understanding is the bridge that connects souls in a world that often desperately needs empathy."

Legacy of the Quiet

"Lives lived softly, with purpose, leave marks deeper than thunder's echo."

Lesson of Humility

"True humility is recognising that every being has something to teach us."

Marathon of Success

"Intelligence may give you a head start, but hard work is the marathon that ensures you cross the finish line."

Mask of Deceit

"Behind the mask of deceit, a liar conceals not just untruths but the profound anxieties that weave the fabric of his fearful heart."

Masterful Giver

"Life is a masterful giver, offering both triumphs and adversities to shape your character and enliven your soul."

Melody of Purpose

"Destiny unfolds its pages, scripted by the ink of our actions. Let every note of action resonate with the melody of a purposeful heart in the symphony of existence."

Modesty and Confidence

"Being modest does not imply a lack of confidence. It implies that you are self-aware enough to recognise and strive to overcome your limitations."

Morning Ritual

"When I wake up early in the morning, I have a cup of coffee to get me going for the day."

Morning Symphony

"An early morning tea, like a cup of joy, invites you to savour the lemony sunrise and the comforting sweetness of honey, a delightful overture to the day's symphony."

Navigating Life's Lows

"Life's true beauty lies not just in its highs, but in the quiet strength found in navigating the lows with resilience and grace."

Navigating Life's Opportunities

"Life's opportunities are not always predictable, but they are exactly what you need to navigate your specific journey and create a meaningful story."

Nourishment of Religion

"Just as water sustains life, religions nourish the soul, providing a sense of purpose and meaning amid the vastness of existence."

Opportunity in Renewal

"A new beginning is not just a chance to start over, but also an opportunity to create something better than before."

Path to True Humanity

"Humility is a quality that leads to wisdom, growth, and respect, and it transforms you into a true human."

Patience for Growth

"When the buds cannot bloom, it serves as a reminder that even the most beautiful things in life require patience, time, and nurturing to thrive."

Patient Endurance

"Even when the buds cannot bloom, the tree stands firm, patiently awaiting its turn."

Perseverance Before Breakthrough

"Never give up, because the moment you feel like giving up could be the moment right before a breakthrough."

Phases of Darkness

"In our brightest moments, we must remember, even the moon has its phases of darkness."

Power of Positive Words

"Words have the ability to change your state of mind. Choose the positive ones, and watch as your surroundings bloom with increased hope and happiness."

Power of Self-Creation

"The closing of a happiness door serves as a reminder that, no matter what our circumstances, we have the power within us to create our happiness."

Power of Transformation

"When we learn to heal and grow from our wounds, we can transform the pain we feel because of them into a source of power and resilience."

Radiant Complexities

"Like the moon's hidden side, our complexities remain concealed beneath our radiant surface."

Reading Unwritten Chapters

"Read the unwritten chapters of someone's soul to understand their essence. The unspoken truths reverberate louder than the scripted words."

Reality Beyond Deceit

"The tangible world is not real; only the intangible is free from deceit."

Redirecting Paths

"When one door of happiness closes, remind yourself that the universe is simply redirecting you to a new and even more fulfilling path."

Reservoir of Humanity

"We find the reservoir of our humanity in the depths of emotion, where joy flows like a river and sorrow like a storm. It is within this profound wellspring that we discover the essence of our shared experience."

Revealing Potential

"Instead of searching for yourself, focus on unveiling your limitless potential and letting your true essence to shine."

Riches of Friendship

"A person with a good friend is rich beyond measure."

Sacred Lessons

"In the pilgrimage of carrying your own water, each drop becomes a sacred lesson, weaving the tapestry of resilience and gratitude within the fabric of your journey."

Savouring Life's Symphony

"The beauty of life lies in the art of emptying your cup, allowing every moment to pour in, and savouring the bittersweet symphony of existence."

Scars of Wisdom

"The scars of our wounds are the road to wisdom, but it's a journey worth taking."

Seed of Resilience

"Within every heartache, rests the seed of resilience."

Seeds of Destiny

"The seeds we plant in the garden of life determine the harvest we reap; sow kindness, and the fruits will be sweet, sow negativity, and the bitter taste shall follow."

Solitude's Echo

"In the solitude of unwavering opinions, one often finds the company of echoing solitude."

Spiritual Rebirth

"Every breath is a chance to be spiritually reborn. But to be reborn into a new life, you must first die."

Spreaders of Sunshine

"The world needs more sunshine bringers - people who spread happiness, love, and joy wherever they go."

Sweetness of Resilience

"Embrace the bitter moments, for within them, the sweetness of resilience is born."

Taste Life's Nectar

"To truly taste the nectar of life, one must first empty their cup of preconceptions and embrace the sweet surprises it offers."

Tenacity Through Twists

"Success rarely follows a straight line. It has a lot of unexpected twists and turns. However, with tenacity and resolve, one can overcome any obstacle."

Threads of Causality

"Our journey through life is a tapestry woven with the threads of causality, where every thought, word, and deed stitches the narrative of our existence, shaping the intricate design of our fate."

Tomorrow's Promise

"The buds may have forgotten to bloom today, but tomorrow is a new day full of new possibilities."

Transformative Humility

"Humility enables us to learn from our mistakes, gracefully acknowledge our accomplishments, and treat others with kindness and compassion."

Transient Realm

"In the transient realm of the material world, everything sensed—fragrance, sound, touch, sight, and taste—is a fleeting manifestation of Prakriti, here for but a moment, gone the next."

Transient Truths

"In the transient dance of moments, a lie may twirl for a mere few hours, but the truth, anchored in eternity, sustains itself through the ages."

Triumph Amidst Trials

"Amid life's trials and tribulations, we find the canvas on which our strength, courage, and determination paint the most captivating stories of triumph."

Turning Within

"True healing starts when we stop turning away and instead turn inward with compassion."

Unearthing Life's Treasures

"We unearth the treasures of life, hidden beneath the surface allure, in the depths of understanding. True worth exists beyond looks."

Unspoken Depths

"The true essence of a person lies not in the words they speak, but in the unspoken depths that echo within their soul."

Value Amid Chaos

"Where is the time for all these trivial things amid chaos and mayhem if you are aware of your mortal nature?"

Wisdom Pearls

"Timeless insights for life are the wisdom pearls we gather along our journey, strung together to illuminate the path for both ourselves and others."

Wisdom and Wounds

"The depth of wisdom can only complement the depth of our wounds we gain from healing them."

Serenity and Balance

Cultivating Inner Peace

"In the heart's stillness, we find the sanctuary of inner peace, a place where life's storms may rage outside, but tranquillity reigns within."

- Shree Shambav

Acceptance of Serenity

"Amidst rage, we forge our shackles, binding ourselves to turmoil." Accept the serenity of your soul, for it is in tranquillity and kindness that we attain true liberation of our being."

Actions Speak Louder

"In a world full of empty promises, let actions be the true measure of one's intentions, as words are frequently used as a pretext."

Avoiding Disappointment

"Expecting perfection in a chaotic world will only lead to disappointment."

Beauty of Imperfect Friendship

"The beauty of friendship lies not in the absence of flaws, but in the acceptance of imperfections, in embracing each other's uniqueness with open hearts."

Beginning of Peace

"Peace begins with a conscious decision to remain calm under all circumstances."

Bliss in Nature's Stillness

"One can discover true bliss in nature's stillness."

Bridges of Words

"Poems on love, diversity, and connection are the bridges we build with words, spanning the divides of culture, race, and creed, reminding us that, in the end, we are all chapters in the same cosmic story."

Clarity in Stillness

"Through the stillness of meditation, we can find the clarity and peace that we seek within ourselves."

Contain Anger, Cultivate Kindness

"Anger, a fleeting firestorm, scalds not only those who come into contact with it but also the vessel that holds it. Allow your heart to be an idyllic garden, nourished by the soothing waters of kindness, where the most exquisite blossoms of your spirit thrive."

Danger of Unrealistic Expectations

"Unrealistic expectations are dangerous because they can prevent you from seeing the situation for what it is."

Delicate Emotions in Stillness

"In the stillness of your contemplation on the Atman, you'll find emotions as delicate as petals, unfolding the secrets of your inner world."

Effecting Positive Change

"Our greatest glory is realising that we can effect positive change in ourselves and the world around us by performing one small act of kindness at a time."

Embrace Forgiveness

"Errors are etched into every story along our shared human journey. To truly thrive, embrace a heart that forgives, forgets, and extends an unwavering arm of support and love to others."

Embrace Life's Paradox

"Embrace life's fascinating paradox, in which struggles become the catalysts that unlock our true potential, leading us to extraordinary experiences and personal evolution."

Embrace Serenity

"Embrace the serenity of silence, for in its depths, you'll discover the Atman's song of love, joy, and profound peace."

Embrace of Nature's Symphony

"Amidst the symphony of life, take a moment to close your eyes, open your heart, and feel the world around you - the whispers of the wind, the warmth of the sun, the aroma of blossoms, the creaking sound of trees, and the embrace of nature's embrace."

Embrace of the Atman

"As you sit quietly and reflect, you'll feel the gentle embrace of the Atman, where emotions flow like rivers, and wisdom rises like the morning sun."

Emotions in the Tapestry of Life

"With every dive into the unknown, emotions become the threads weaving the pearls of experience in the tapestry of life."

Empowerment of Freedom

"Freedom is not only the absence of chains but also the empowerment to forge one's path, guided by the compass of choice and the wings of self-expression."

Ending Greed and Fear

"Destroy your desire to end greed and destroy greed to end fear."

Extent of Ignorance

"To know the extent of one's ignorance... It is poverty that causes a rich man to despise the poor, and it is ignorance that causes a wise man to despise the ignorant. Even the owner of ignorance is an enemy. Ignorance despises knowledge because it is unadulterated."

Finding Peace in Nature

"The woods are a place to get away from the chaos of the outside world and find peace in the simplicity of nature."

Gentle Music of the Soul

"Inner peace is the gentle music of the soul, and when we tune in with mindfulness and self-compassion, we harmonise our existence with the universe's eternal symphony."

Gratitude for Awakening

"I was in a delusion; I am grateful for bringing me out of the dark cloud of ignorance."

Guardians of Life

"With weathered hands and a heart full of hope, the farmer becomes a guardian of life. Through sweat and toil, they cultivate the seeds that nourish not only their bodies but also their souls, embodying a sacred dance with the earth."

Happiness as a Masterpiece

"In the tapestry of life, the division is the thread woven by human hands, but true happiness is the masterpiece painted by the heart's contentment."

Harnessing Collective Consciousness

"The power of collective consciousness is undeniable; harness it, and you'll gain access to a force that has the potential to change the world."

Heart's Song

"A friend is someone who knows the lyrics to your heart song and can sing it back to you when you can't remember the words."

Influence of Company

"Who we are is determined by the company we keep. 'Surround yourself with people that reflect who you want to be and how you want to feel.' Energies are contagious."

Inner Glory

"Our greatest glory is not seeking external validation, but nurturing the inner light that illuminates brightly from within."

Inner Peace in Doing Right

"Doing the right thing will always bring you inner peace and a clear conscience, even if it is not always the easiest course of action."

Interconnected Heartbeats

"Our heartbeats may appear distinct, but they are all intertwined in the symphony of life."

Journey of Reflections

"Life's journey is a tapestry of reflections, each moment a thread in the intricate weave of our existence, revealing the beauty and wisdom hidden within the fabric of time."

Live Each Moment Fully

"Unrealistic expectations can lead to a life of constant discontent and uneasiness."

Love's Conundrum

"Love is a conundrum that the heart delights in solving, a puzzle that is solved with each heartbeat."

Love's Enigma

"The enigma of love is written in the stars, whispered by the wind, and sensed in the depths of our souls."

Managing Expectations

"Expecting too much from others is a surefire way to be let down."

Merge with Self-Awareness

"As you sit quietly and reflect on the Atman, let your emotions flow like rivers, merging with the boundless ocean of self-awareness, where every feeling finds its home."

Moonlight's Soothing Embrace

"Moonlight, the mystic smile of the night, can soothe the soul and calm the mind."

Mosaic of Life

"Life is a mosaic of fascinating moments intertwined with threads of struggle, serving as a constant reminder that our victories result from our ability to overcome obstacles."

Overcoming Regret

"Regret stems from hesitations and missed opportunities. So, take a confident step forward, give it your all, and let your potential shine."

Payoff of a Tough Road

"A tough road is never a peaceful journey, but the payoff at the end is well worth it."

Perils of Unrealistic Expectations

"Unrealistic expectations are perilous because they are never met."

Perseverance Towards Success

"The road to success is long and winding, but with perseverance and patience, we will get there eventually."

Perseverance in Adversity

"In the face of adversity, keep moving forward with unwavering resolve. Your perseverance will pave the way for success."

Perseverance in Uncertainty

"When faced with uncertainty, fear, or doubt, remember to give it your all. Your perseverance and resilience will lead to extraordinary results."

Power of Stillness

"In the gentle hush of stillness, we find the power to heal, the clarity to see, and the grace to truly be."

Premeditated Resentment

"Expectations are premeditated resentment and anger."

Profound Movements in Stillness

"By practising stillness, we learn that the most profound movements in life often occur within the quiet spaces of our hearts."

Progress through Faith

"Your trials keep you strong and determined. Oh! human, you encounter sorrows that will keep you agile and alive! In turn, failure teaches you humility! After realising the truth, you will continue to shine because of your success! Faith is the only thing that keeps you continuously progressing."

Progressive Journey

"Life is a journey that necessitates progress. Keep moving, because each step brings you closer to your goals."

Promise of Growth

"In the ominous shadow of the dark cloud before the pouring rain, we find the promise of growth, resilience, and the beauty of a fresh start."

Reflect on Inner Peace

"Sit quietly and reflect on the Atman, for within its depths, you'll discover the ocean of serenity that can calm even the stormiest of emotions."

Reflection of Worth

"A true friend is like a mirror, reflecting the best parts of yourself and reminding you of your worth when you forget."

Revealing Profound Essence

"Salt and camphor, which appear to be mere grains, reveal their profound essence upon closer inspection. Just as the mysteries of life emerge in layers, each soul has a distinct melody beneath the surface symphony."

Seeds of Expectation

"The seeds of expectation sprout the vines of reliance, which, if left unchecked, transform into thorns of burdens and tangles of entanglement."

Serenity Amid Chaos

"Serenity is inner peace amidst chaos and trouble, not their absence."

Soul's Compass

"The soul is the compass of our existence. We navigate the vast landscape of our dreams and desires by nourishing our souls with love, creativity, and purpose."

Soul's Language

"Deep silence is the soul's language, where words are unnecessary, and the heart speaks the truth."

Stagnant Hate, Free-flowing Love

"Hate is like stagnant water; love is like a free-flowing stream. Never be stagnant water as it causes mental, bodily, and emotional suffering."

Stillness of Nature

"You'll find a place deep in the woods where time stands still and the beauty of nature is all that matters."

Strength Amid Chaos

"Learn to stay calm amidst the chaos to find the strength to navigate through any storm."

Strength in Silence

"In times of profound silence, we find the stillness to hear our inner voice and the strength to heed it."

Symbol of Hope

"When a shooting star crosses your path, let it be a symbol of hope, reminding you that your wishes can come true."

Timeless Insights in the Tapestry

"In the tapestry of existence, timeless insights are woven with threads of experience, creating a masterpiece of profound understanding."

Tranquil Harbour of Patience

"Amidst the storm of anger, the tranquil harbour of patience is the anchor that prevents the shipwreck of a hundred subsequent regrets."

Tranquillity of Serenity

"Serenity is the tranquillity of an undisturbed soul, the calmness of a peaceful mind, and the stillness of a quiet heart."

Unity of Hearts

"Our hearts beat in unison, in time, with the rhythm of life."

Unlocking the Soul's Sanctuary

"By practising stillness, we discover the calm within us and unlock the door to our soul's sanctuary, where serenity and wisdom reside."

Unrealistic Expectations and Failure

"Unrealistic expectations are the seeds of failure."

Whispers of the Atman

"In the stillness of a quiet moment, allow your soul to speak, and you will find the Atman, the eternal self, whispering its truths."

Success and Achievement
Unleashing Your Potential

"Unleashing your potential is like releasing a caged bird; it soars to unimaginable heights, painting the sky with the vibrant colours of your dreams."

- Shree Shambav

Actions Speak Louder

"In a world that can be confusing and chaotic, let your actions speak louder than your words by consistently choosing to do the right thing."

Adversity as a Sculptor of Character

"The adversity of obstacles, which are the chisels that sculpt our character, gives us the strength to evolve into the masterpiece of our potential."

Anomalies in Exceptional Circumstances

"Anomalies are not outliers. They result from exceptional circumstances that benefit them."

Beauty of Doing the Right Thing

"The beauty of doing the right thing lies in the growth and strength it cultivates within yourself, as well as the positive impact it has on others."

Breaking Free from Stagnation

"Breaking free from the shackles of stagnation, don't tether your spirit to the heavy millstone of inertia."

Collective Reward

"The best reward comes from our collective effort and energy."

Combination of Success

"The true measure of success lies in the combination of intelligence and hard work, for one cannot replace the other."

Common Roots

"The wings of time may carry us on diverse journeys, but the common roots we share will always guide us back to the same ground."

Conquering Fear

"Fear of failure is natural, but don't let it cloud your potential. Accept the unknown, take calculated risks, and let your bravery shine."

Consequences of Actions

"The resounding proclamation, 'I am well-versed in every subject,' resonates with self-confidence, but within the corridors of selfhood, the doer cannot escape the shadows of consequences that follow every action."

Consistency in Righteousness

"Do the right thing not because it is easy, but because it is consistent with the person you want to be."

Continuous Progress

"The key to reaching your destination is to keep moving, no matter how small the steps appear. Progress is progress, regardless of size."

Courage in Adversity

"When things get tough, remember that stagnation breeds complacency. Embrace your courage and keep moving towards your goals."

Creating Possibilities

"Lateral thinking is about creating new possibilities, not just finding solutions to existing problems."

Don't waste precious moments

"The journey is fleeting, so don't waste precious moments. Embrace the present while keeping your eyes on the future."

Elixir of Life

"The elixir of life is not a substance to be discovered, but a way of being that must be developed. The things that keep us alive are mental, physical, and spiritual balance, the quest for knowledge and wisdom, and acts of kindness and compassion."

Embracing Opportunities

"When you give up, you close the door on opportunities you may not have realised existed."

Embracing Progress

"Every step of your journey is an opportunity for growth and discovery. Instead of lingering, embrace the momentum of progress."

Embracing the Present

"In the grand scheme of existence, our trials and tribulations are as transient as dust and ashes. Embrace and make the present meaningful."

Empowerment of Mind and Spirit

"Empowering the mind and spirit is the journey to free ourselves from the shackles of limitation, allowing us to soar on the wings of our potential."

Endless Learning and Growth

"Just as learning has no end, so does growth."

Essential Life Lessons

"Although life's lessons aren't always easy, they are essential for our personal growth."

Eternal Symphony of Growth

"In the boundless journey of learning, growth unfolds its petals without an end, echoing the eternal symphony of human evolution."

Exploring Creativity

"Exploring the unexpected and coming up with new, creative ideas are at the heart of lateral thinking."

Failure and Success

"Failure is an essential component of success; it is not the inverse of success. Accept it, learn from it, and use it to your advantage."

Forge Unyielding Strength

"In the crucible of life, standing firm without letting emotions sway is the alchemy that forges unyielding strength."

Fullness of Purpose and Passion

"Shake off the emptiness of life, and let the echoes of your essence reverberate with the fullness of purpose and passion."

Growth Through Challenges

"Challenges teach you to be more responsible. Always remember that without struggle, there is no growth."

Guidance of the Moral Compass

"When faced with a choice, let your moral compass guide you towards doing the right thing, for it is a compass that never steers you wrong."

Guiding Light in Adversity

"Faced with adversity, don't lose your heart; instead, let it be your guiding light and source of strength."

Hope in Darkness

"Even on the darkest of nights, a single candle can light up a room and bring hope."

Importance of Lateral Thinking

"The key to creativity and innovation is lateral thinking."

Journey of Self-Creation

"Life isn't about finding yourself; it's about creating yourself and embracing the journey of self-discovery."

Journey of Self-Discovery

"The true beauty of life lies in the realisation that it's not about finding yourself, but about embracing the journey of self-discovery and growth."

Journey vs. Destination

"While standing on the summit, we are reminded that the journey is just as important as the destination because the lessons we learn along the way shape who we are."

Later Thinking

"To engage in lateral thinking, one must let go of preconceived notions and consider novel concepts."

Learning from Adversity

"Life isn't always fair, but it always teaches us something. We must learn from our mistakes and use them to strengthen ourselves."

Leaving an Indelible Mark

"Burn brightly, even if it means going down in flames because the intensity of your fire will leave an indelible imprint on the world."

Legacy in the Interim

"We rise from the dust and fall to the ashes, but what matters is the legacy we leave behind in the interim."

Life Lessons

"Life lessons are not always taught in school. They are occasionally exposed to the 'school of hard knocks.'"

Literature as Journey

"Indulging in literature is akin to setting off on a journey to a distant land. It expands our horizons, dares us to question our preconceptions, and enhances our perception of the world. It is a gateway into the human psyche, granting us access to the pleasures, adversities, and intricacies of the human condition."

Meaningful Life

"Seek not the superficial allure of fame, but the deep satisfaction of living a purposeful and meaningful life."

Obstacles as Threads of Character

"Obstacles are the threads of character in the tapestry of life. Our story becomes more intricate and beautiful as we weave between them."

Opening Doors to Possibilities

"Empowering the mind is like opening a door to limitless possibilities, whereas nurturing the spirit is like lighting a fire that illuminates the path to self-discovery."

Overcoming Fear of Failure

"The only true failure is allowing fear of failure to prevent you from acting and pursuing your dreams."

Passion and Enthusiasm

"The road to greatness is paved with the bricks of passion and the mortar of enthusiasm. Without these fuels, the fire within remains dormant, and the pursuit of dreams becomes a mere flicker in the vast darkness of potential."

Passion as a Lifelong Journey

"To pursue one's passions is to embark on a lifelong love affair with the heart, a journey where the soul finds its truest expression in the dance of dreams realised."

Perspective Shift

"Lateral thinking is the ability to see things from a different perspective, often leading to breakthroughs and discoveries."

Power of Healing in the Heart

"Remember that your heart has the power to heal, persevere, and find joy again in times of despair."

Power of Mind

"Your mind is like a magnet, drawing thoughts and experiences that are consistent with your beliefs and emotions."

Power of Positive Thinking

"Always think positively to attract positivity into your life, because your mind is a magnet that attracts what you think about."

Pursuing True Glory

"Instead of chasing empty promises of fame, seek the fulfilment and meaning that come from pursuing true glory."

Reflection in Introspection

"In the mirror of introspection, we find the reflection of our true self, and in the journey to understand it, we uncover the purpose that gives our life meaning."

Resilience of the Human Spirit

"The flickering flame of a candle represents the human spirit's resilience, capable of withstanding even the strongest winds."

Respect for Individual Spiritual Paths

"Don't pass judgment on how humans communicate with the Supreme because everyone has their way of doing things."

Rewriting Your Story

"Don't let societal expectations define your worth or capabilities based on your age; remember, you are never too old to rewrite your story and create a legacy."

Rising from Adversity

"Sometimes, you have to be willing to go down in flames to rise from the ashes and become stronger than ever."

Silent Symphony of Character

"In the ephemeral theatre of reputation, applause is fleeting, and criticism is but a passing breeze. Character, on the other hand, is the silent symphony that continues to play, leaving a lasting melody in the hearts of those who truly understand its depth."

Solace in Simplicity

"We find solace and peace in the light of a candle, a gentle reminder to slow down and appreciate the little things in life."

Strength in Adversity

"Don't be afraid to go down in flames, for it is only in the heat of the fire that you discover what truly matters and find the strength to rise again."

Struggles Add Depth

"The struggles we face add depth, meaning, and richness to the remarkable story of our lives in the intricate tapestry of existence."

Success and Lateral Thinking

"The most successful people are those who think outside of the box and embrace lateral thinking."

Tapestry of Self-Mastery

"The art of strength lies in controlling others, but the true masterpiece is woven in the tapestry of self-mastery, the mark of genuine power."

Transformations in Life

"Life's transformations are the chisel and the canvas, shaping us into the masterpiece we're meant to become."

True Elixir of Life

"The pursuit of the elixir of life may be eternal, but the true elixir lies within us - in the moments we cherish, the connections we make, and the memories we create."

True Glory

"True glory is found in the pursuit of excellence, the embodiment of values, and the positive impact you have on others."

True Measure of Glory

"The true measure of glory is found in the character you cultivate and your positive impact on the world, not in fleeting fame."

Uncharted Exploration

"A ship is not meant to be anchored in the safety of a harbour. It is intended to explore the vastness of the ocean, to contend with unpredictable winds and waves, and to discover new horizons."

Value of the Heart

"Value your heart, for it is the source of all courage, compassion, and unwavering hope."

Visibility of Outliers

"Outliers are not necessarily uncommon; they are simply not always visible."

The Beauty of Simplicity

Embracing Life's Little Pleasures

"We find the warmth of contentment in the embrace of life's little pleasures, like a cosy blanket on a chilly day, wrapping us in simple joy."

- *Shree Shambav*

A Prayer of Presence

"Healing begins when we see our body with gratitude, not judgment, and choose to stay."

Alchemy of Flavours

"In the gentle steam rising from an early morning cup, we discover the alchemy of lemon's zest and honey's nectar, crafting a symphony of flavours that dances on the palate."

Appreciating Life's Beauty

"I went for a walk - through the woods and fields, the coastline and rivers, the mountains and sea, and the earth and sky. I realised that life is full of beauty after seeing the flying bees, the fragrance of flowers, the smell of rain, the soft touch of the wind, the roaring waves, and the flashing stars."

Appreciating Miracles

"Miracles happen every day, but we often miss them because we're too preoccupied with looking for grandiose signs rather than appreciating the small wonders that surround us."

Appreciating Simple Pleasures

"Some of the best things in life are free, and one of them is fresh air. So go outside, take a deep breath, and appreciate life's simple pleasures."

Attitude Determines Happiness

"The key to happiness is to change your attitude rather than your circumstances. Decide to be upbeat rather than miserable."

Beauty in Struggle and Triumph

"Life's true beauty lies in the fascinating interplay of struggle and triumph, for it is only through our challenges that we discover our strength."

Bright Moon and Shadowed Realm

"We are like the bright moon in the vast expanse of existence, luminous and captivating. Yet there is a shadowed realm within us, a quieter reflection that adds depth to our brilliance."

Celestial Melodies

"As the moon whispers melodies, the stars twirl in a celestial waltz upon the tranquil ripples."

Character Reflects Actions

"Our character is measured not by what we say, but by what we do. Doing the right thing reflects our true nature."

Choosing Happiness

"A pessimistic outlook only serves to spread pessimism. Choose happiness and positivity instead."

Choosing Righteousness

"Doing the right thing may not always be the easiest or most popular choice, but it is the choice that will bring us peace and fulfilment in the end."

Collecting Treasures of Joy

"Finding joy in the present moment is like collecting treasures along the shores of time, for it is in these precious moments that we discover the true riches of our existence."

Commitment to Doing Right

"We owe it to ourselves and others to do the right thing, no matter how difficult it is."

Contemplating Life's Footprints

"Reflections on life's journey are the moments when we pause to contemplate the path behind us, finding in our memories the footprints of who we were and the roadmaps to who we can become."

Continuous Learning and Growth

"Just as learning has no end, so does growth."

Cosmic Symphony

"When the universe orchestrates its symphony, stars become dancers on the ripples of cosmic music."

Courage to Embrace Freedom

"It takes courage to let go of the past, but the ability to forget it is where true freedom is found."

Dance in the Rain

"When life throws you curveballs, embrace them and dance gracefully in the raindrops."

Dancing in Life's Challenges

"Life isn't about waiting for the storm to pass; it's about learning to dance in the rain."

Dancing in Resilience

"Don't let the rain dampen your spirit; instead, allow it to be the music that guides your dance of resilience and growth."

Earth's Laughter

"The Earth laughs at the innocence of children, the playfulness of animals and birds, and the wonder of discovery, all of which are reflections of the pure and simple joys that life offers."

Earth's Resilience

"The Earth beams in the face of adversity, proving that even in the most difficult times, beauty, hope, and resilience can be found."

Embrace Puddle-Wonderful Moments

"When life gives you a puddle, jump in with both feet and embrace the puddle-wonderful moments."

Embracing Infinite Possibilities

"In the void, there is the potential for infinite possibilities. Allow life to write its beautiful story on you as an empty page."

Embracing Life's Cozy Blanket

"Life's little pleasures are the tender threads of warmth that weave a cosy blanket around our souls, shielding us from the chill of the mundane and inviting us to bask in the simple joy of existence."

Embracing Life's Richness

"Life is too short to settle for mediocrity; challenge yourself to step outside of your comfort zone and do something wonderful that fills your days with purpose and fulfilment."

Empty Page of Life

"Be an empty page, ready to be filled with the stories of your dreams, the hues of your experiences, and the wisdom of your journey."

Enriching Generosity

"Generosity enriches the spirit, while pride impoverishes the soul."

Eternal Symphony of Growth

"In the boundless journey of learning, growth unfolds its petals without an end, echoing the eternal symphony of human evolution."

Exhilaration and Terror

"Life, like the wind, can be exhilarating and terrifying at the same time, but it is in the face of these challenges that we grow the most."

Faith as a Guardian Knot

"Like a guardian knot in the fabric of the universe, faith binds our hearts unyieldingly, infusing our emotions with the depth and resilience needed to navigate the cosmic symphony of life."

Faith as a Guiding Light

"Faith, the guardian knot of the human spirit, unwavering amidst cosmic ebb and flow, is the wellspring of our profound emotions, guiding us through the boundless depths of existence."

Father's Love as Encouragement

"Father's love, like the wind's unseen force, whispers words of encouragement and pushes us to reach new heights."

Fear as a Guidepost

"Fear is not your adversary; rather, it serves as a guidepost pointing you towards the challenges you must face and overcome in your quest for growth."

Fearlessness and Courage

"Being fearless does not imply being courageous. It implies that you continue despite your fear."

Finding Joy in Storms

"Find your rhythm and learn to dance joyfully on the wet path amid life's storms."

Finding Profound Richness

"In the simplicity of life's pleasures, we discover the profound richness of our existence, where the ordinary becomes extraordinary, and every moment is a celebration of the human spirit."

Focus on Joy

"Avoid squandering your energy on misery and negativity. Concentrate on what makes you joyful."

Fuelling Determination

"Don't let the fear of failure paralyse you; instead, use it to fuel your determination and push you to take bold risks and reach new heights."

Hidden Blessings

"Embrace what life gives you, for even the unexpected can hold hidden blessings and opportunities."

Hidden Gems of Life

"Life's little pleasures are the hidden gems of our existence, just waiting to be discovered in the tapestry of everyday moments."

Innate Inequalities

"Although the concept of equal opportunity is admirable, it cannot address the innate inequalities that exist from birth."

Inner Source of Resilience

"When I looked deep within myself, I discovered a source of courage and resilience."

Joy as Magic

"Joy is the magical ingredient that gives your smile a dash of magic and authenticity."

Joy as a Shield

"When you carry joy in your heart, it becomes a shield against negativity, empowering you to rise above challenges and embrace life with optimism."

Joy in the Present

"In the garden of now, joy is the vibrant bloom we pluck, its fragrance a reminder that life's beauty is woven into each passing moment."

Joyful Heart

"If you carry joy in your heart, you become a beacon of light in a world that desperately needs positivity and love."

Leading Lives of Integrity

"Embracing who we truly are and leading lives of passion, purpose, and integrity will bring us the greatest glory."

Leaving a Trail of Wonder

"Leave a trail of wonder in your wake, knowing that every step you take has the potential to lead to something truly magnificent."

Life's Growth

"Life may not always give you what you want, but it will always give you what you need to grow."

Life's Possibilities

"Life is like a puddle; it can be dull and unremarkable or puddle-wonderful, with limitless possibilities."

Magic of Fresh Air

"The beauty of fresh air is that it's always there, just waiting for us to take a deep breath and let it work its magic."

Morning's Blend of Joy

"Sip the morning's first cup of joy, where lemony whispers meet the sweet embrace of honey, and you'll find the perfect blend to awaken your day."

Overflowing Generosity

"Generosity overflows when you give beyond your limits, and humility shines in taking only what's necessary."

Passion and Enthusiasm as Building Blocks

"The road to greatness is paved with the bricks of passion and the mortar of enthusiasm. Without these fuels, the fire within remains dormant, and the pursuit of dreams becomes a mere flicker in the vast darkness of potential."

Planting Hope

"Planting a tree is more than just an act of hope; it's a pledge to future generations that we cared enough to make a difference, one tree at a time."

Profound Beauty of Life

"The world may dazzle with surface glimmer, but the profound beauty of life lies beneath. During our exploratory adventure, we uncover our most precious treasures."

Puddle-Wonderful Moments

"Puddle-wonderful moments are like rainbows after the storm. They remind us that there is beauty in every situation."

Remedy of Fresh Air

"A walk in the fresh air is the perfect remedy for a troubled mind, as it helps us gain perspective and find peace within."

Reviving Spirits

"Fresh air, the elixir of life, revives our spirits and nourishes our bodies."

Secrets of Nature

"Nature's secrets are simplicity and patience."

Self-Confidence and Consequences

"The resounding proclamation, 'I am well-versed in every subject,' resonates with self-confidence, but within the corridors of selfhood, the doer cannot escape the shadows of consequences that follow every action."

Self-Mastery

"The art of strength lies in controlling others, but the true masterpiece is woven in the tapestry of self-mastery, the mark of genuine power."

Singing Odes to the Earth

"In the verses of odes to the Earth, we sing timeless ballads of our profound connection to this sacred land, where echoes of nature's wisdom and the rhythms of existence intertwine."

Smile as a Blossoming Flower

"In the depths of your joy, your smile blossoms like a flower, spreading warmth and happiness to all who witness it."

Smile as a Source of Joy

"Your smile opens the door to joy, bringing more happiness and optimism into your life."

Solace in Nature's Embrace

"Beyond the rush of existence, find solace in the simple act of feeling the world around you—the earth's pulse beneath your feet, the melodies carried by birds, the aroma spread by blossoms, and stories whispered by the breeze."

Spreading Wonder and Inspiration

"You have the power to spread wonder and inspiration far beyond your existence. Accept it and let your actions speak for themselves."

Stars Dancing on Dreams

"Stars descend to dance upon the ripples of dreams in the still embrace of the night."

Tenacity Prevails

"Challenges and setbacks frequently line the path to our greatest glory, but it is only through tenacity that we prevail."

The Beauty of Nature's Simplicity

"Nature is beautiful because it is simple."

The Dance of Freedom

"Like a flying kite dance in the wind, freedom finds its beauty in the harmony of restraint and liberation, a delicate dance between control and the boundless sky."

The Living Frame

"Your body is no mere structure, but a garden nurtured by how you see and care for it."

The Question Within

"Beneath the surface lies a quiet question: do you truly know your own body?"

Trusting Life's Journey

"When one door of happiness closes, trust in the ebb and flow of life's journey and have faith that new doors will open, leading you to greater fulfilment."

Unleashing Potential with Commitment

"You have the potential to create something truly wonderful when you fully commit yourself to what you love. Do not be afraid to dream big and follow your dreams."

Veiled Treasures of Life

"To fathom the essence of life's beauty, we must plunge beneath the superficial. Real treasures are veiled, waiting to be discovered by those who dare to explore."

Vitality of Fresh Air

"Taking a deep breath of fresh air is like taking a shot of pure vitality; it awakens our senses and fills us with energy."

Words Become Roots

"The words you speak to your body take root—be mindful whether they nurture or harm."

Nature Symphony
Odes to the Earth

"The Earth's odes are written in nature's language, sung by the birds, and painted in the seasons' colours, a love song to the planet we call home."

- *Shree Shambav*

Antidote of Fresh Air

"Fresh air is the perfect antidote to stress and anxiety, as it calms the mind and soothes the soul."

Awakening with Sunrise

"With each sunrise, let your heart awaken, ready to embrace the day's blessings and share the gift of love."

Awe-Inspiring Fairness of Nature

"Nature's fairness is awe-inspiring, but her beauty is enthralling."

Awe-inspiring Shooting Stars

"As shooting stars streak across the sky, they inspire awe and wonder in us, reminding us of the vastness of the universe."

Beauty in Simplicity

"Nature is beautiful because it is simple."

Beauty in the Surroundings

"Look around you for a moment. You'll be surprised at how much beauty you've been missing."

Beneath the Still Waters

"Potential sleeps beneath the calm surface, waiting not for permission, but for courage. Stir the waters, and the depths within you will awaken the tides."

Boundless Freedom of the Wind

"In the boundless sky, the wind knows no boundaries; it flows freely, seeking solace in the embrace of nature's mysteries."

Breathtaking Growth Among Trees

"Being surrounded by trees serves as a constant reminder that, while growth is a slow process, the outcomes can be breathtaking."

Butterflies as Art

"Butterflies are living works of art, exhibiting the vibrant hues and delicate intricacies that exist in nature's aesthetics."

Cleansing Grace of Rain

"Feel the shivers of vulnerability in the rain, a gentle reminder that even in discomfort, nature's tears bestow a cleansing grace upon the soul."

Cosmic Awe of Shooting Stars

"A shooting star streaks across the sky, lighting up our dreams with a brief flash of cosmic awe."

Cosmic Ballet of Existence

"All entities, whether lifeless or alive, gracefully waltz through the cosmic ballet of birth, existence, and eventual dissolution in the grand theatre of the universe."

Cosmic Precision and Beauty

"The cosmos is a masterpiece of precision, a symphony of order and beauty."

Cosmic Whispers of Shooting Stars

"Shooting stars carry the secrets of the cosmos, whispering tales of distant galaxies and untold wonders."

Dark Clouds and Renewal

"The dark cloud before the pouring rain reminds us that storms are temporary, but the nourishing waters of hope and renewal are everlasting."

Dawn's Gentle Awakening

"Amidst the tranquil dawn, the sun's gentle rays breathe life into dew-kissed leaves, a reminder that beauty awakens in subtlety."

Earth's Joyous Chuckles

"The Earth chuckles in the sun's warmth, the coolness of the rain, and the majesty of the mountains, a testament to the wonder and diversity of our planet."

Earth's Laughter

"The Earth laughs in the rustle of leaves and the sound of the wind, a gentle reminder that nature is always alive and vibrant."

Earth's Silent Poetry

"We witness the Earth's silent poetry, etched in light, every dawn, as the sun's soft rays caress dew-covered leaves."

Echoes of Life's Dance

"In the rhythmic cadence of nature's cycle, we find echoes of our own eternal dance through the tapestry of life."

Embrace Fear to Soar

"Embrace your fear of falling and transform it into the courage to soar if you want to fly."

Embrace What Lifts You

"If you want to fly, let go of what's holding you down and embrace what lifts you."

Embracing Rain's Dance

"Embrace the rain in the dance of life, for it weaves the melody of acceptance and the rhythm of resilience."

Enchantment of the Woods

"The woods are a place of mystery and enchantment, with light dancing through the leaves and shadows playing mind games."

Equitable Balance of Nature

"Nature strives for balance by giving and taking equitably."

Equity in Nature

"The equity of nature resides because every living creature possesses an equal entitlement to survive and flourish."

Escape to Nature's Simplicity

"When I walk into the wild, I leave behind the world's noise and chaos and enter a realm of simplicity and marvel."

Ever-changing Yet Constant Sky

"The clouds may change shape and move, but the sky remains an infinite canvas of possibility."

Fairness and Beauty of Nature

"Nature's ability to sustain life for all is the epitome of her fairness, which is only surpassed by her mesmerising beauty."

Fairness in Nature's Balance

"The fairest thing about nature is not its beauty, but her balance."

Finding Solace Among Trees

"Amid the daily chaos, spending time among trees reminds us to slow down, breathe deeply, and appreciate the beauty of the world."

Fireflies' Symphony of Light

"As the sun sets, fireflies take centre stage, creating a symphony of light that captures hearts and minds."

Fleeting Moments of Life

"Life is like the blowing wind, ever-changing and unpredictable, reminding us that in its fleeting moments, we find the beauty of both turbulence and serenity."

Flight of Gratitude

"At dawn, let your heart take flight in gratitude, soaring through the day on the wings of love."

Floral Enticement

"Flowers' fragrance entices insects to hum in their midst."

Flowers of Wisdom Amidst Adversity

"The seeds of growth are planted in the rich soil of adversity. With perseverance, life's hardships can be transformed into flowers of wisdom."

Gift of Fresh Air

"Fresh air is nature's way of reminding us that every breath is a gift."

Graceful Dance of Paddy Fields

"In the tranquil embrace of a gentle breeze, paddy fields dance with grace, a symphony of nature's poetry."

Gratitude at Dawn

"As the sun kisses the horizon, let your heart soar with gratitude, for each dawn is a precious gift, a canvas awaiting the brushstrokes of love."

Gratitude at Sunrise

"With each sunrise, let your heart soar with the wings of gratitude, weaving a symphony of appreciation for the boundless opportunities to love and be loved."

Harmonious Chorus of Birds

"The air resonates with the harmonious chorus of birds, their dance on branches an ode to the timeless symphony of existence."

Harmonious Chorus of the Forest

"Amidst the tranquil forest, the harmonious chorus of birds flitting from branch to branch fills the air, painting a portrait of serenity and life's continuous rhythm."

Harmony in Nature's Coexistence

"Nature's fairest feature is how everything coexists in harmony with one another."

Hopeful Sunrise

"The gorgeous sunrise is the one that gives you hope in your heart and gives you another day to pursue your dreams."

Immersing in Nature's Vibrance

"Take a deep breath and immerse yourself in nature. Everything around you will be colourful."

Importance of Every Living Creature

"The fairest thing about nature is that every living creature, no matter how big or small, is equally important."

Inspiration from Fireflies

"Fireflies, with their humble brilliance, inspire and uplift our spirits, reminding us to cherish the simple pleasures in life."

Journey of the Wind

"Ask not where the wind goes, for it dances with the leaves, plays with the waves, and caresses the mountains—forever on a journey of endless wonder."

Leaf's Journey

"The fall of a leaf is not the end of its journey, but the beginning of something greater."

Life's Melody in Symphony

"In the grand symphony of existence, life is the melody carried by the blowing wind, a dance of joy and sorrow, a song of love and longing."

Life's Resemblance to the Wind

"Life is like the blowing wind, sometimes gentle and caressing, other times fierce and unrelenting, but always filled with moments that take your breath away."

Magic of Fireflies

"The gentle glow of fireflies, which carries the magic of childhood dreams, sparks our sense of wonder and nostalgia."

Magical World of Fireflies

"In the presence of fireflies, the world transforms into a magical wonderland, where the mundane becomes extraordinary."

Majestic Power of the Ocean

"The roaring waves crash against the shore, creating a symphony of sound and motion, a constant reminder of the ocean's vastness and power."

Morning's Melodic Symphony

"In the morning's tender light, the harmonious chorus of birds hopping from branch to branch fills the air, a melody of nature's awakening."

Nature's Equitable Role

"Nature is fair in the sense that every living creature has a role to play in the grand scheme of things."

Nature's Generosity

"The fairest thing about nature is that she always provides, even when we take more than we give."

Nature's Lesson on Equality

"The fairest thing about nature is that she shows us the true meaning of equality and diversity."

Nature's Masterpiece

"The wild is a canvas on which nature paints its masterpiece, and I am fortunate to witness it unfold."

Nature's Quietude

"The departure of the wind brings stillness to the skies, grounding kites, settling dry leaves, and rendering trees as mere observers of the world's quietude."

Nature's Symphony of Gravitation

"Kites fall from grace, dry leaves submit to gravity, and trees stand as silent sentinels awaiting the gentle flutter of its embrace in the absence of the wind."

Nature's Thunderous Symphony

"Thunder rumbles and echoes through the mountains, reminding us of nature's raw power and beauty."

New Beginnings in the Withering Wind

"The withering wind may bring storms and devastation, but it also clears the way for new beginnings."

Nurturing Promise

"When you plant a tree, you are committing to both the soil and the timeless lessons of patience. In this poetic pact with nature, each tender shoot whispers the promise of a new beginning."

Overcoming Limitations

"Your only limitation is your willingness, which prevents you from exceeding your limit."

Playful Embrace of Rain

"The embrace of playfulness is found in the rain, where each drop carries the joy of spontaneity and the promise of renewal."

Puddle-Wonderful Reflections

"Puddles are nature's canvas, creating puddle-wonderful reflections of the world."

Puddle-Wonderful World

"The world is a puddle-wonderful place, full of unexpected beauty and joy just waiting to be discovered."

Realising Your Potential

"If you push yourself to do something extraordinary, you'll realise how incredible you are."

Reminder of Life's Motion

"The blowing wind reminds us that life is always in motion, and we don't always have control over where it takes us."

Renewal and Growth with Drizzle

"The drizzle reminds us that, while life isn't always sunny, it is still necessary for renewal and growth."

Renewal in the Wind's Withering

"The withering wind blows away the old leaves, making way for the new ones to emerge."

Revealing Nature's Jewellery

"In the early morning, the sun's gentle rays, glistening on dew-kissed leaves, reveal nature's intricate jewellery."

Revitalising Fresh Air

"Fresh air revitalises and rejuvenates our entire being, like a healing balm for the soul."

Secrets Whispered to the Wind

"As the gentle breeze caresses the paddy fields, they sway in harmonious rhythm, whispering secrets to the wind."

Secrets of Nature

"Nature's secret is simplicity and patience."

Secrets of the Woods

"Deep in the woods, you'll discover a world of magic and wonder, where forest life forms wander freely, and trees whisper ancient secrets."

Shine like a Butterfly

"Like a butterfly, let your inner beauty shine, for it is only by embracing your distinctive colours that you inspire others to do the same."

Significance of the Drizzle

"The drizzle reminds us that even seemingly insignificant things can have a significant impact on our lives and that the most beautiful things can come from the most unexpected places."

Solace in Dawn's Light

"In the embrace of dawn's light, find solace in the symphony of existence, where gratitude becomes the melody that dances through your awakened heart."

Symphony of Raindrops

"Raindrops dance across the surface of the puddle, creating a puddle-wonderful symphony of sound."

The Caged Flame

"You were not born to flicker in shadows. You are a flame meant to rise, to light the sky—not by chance, but by choice, to burn beyond your boundaries."

The Mountain Within

"The greatest obstacle is not the storm outside, but the voice within that says you cannot climb. Yet with every trembling step taken in faith, the mountain loses power, and your spirit gains its peak."

The Seed Remembers the Sun

"Inside every hesitation lies a seed aching for growth. Even in darkness, it remembers the sun—because what you are meant to become is already within you."

Threads of Balance

"In the grand tapestry of existence, threads of control and threads of release weave together the fabric of our days. Embrace the dance between what we can influence and what we must allow to flow, for therein lies the poetry of a balanced life."

Thrill of Nature's Elements

"Meadows would bore without greenery, and woods would be silent without birds and insects. There would have been no thrill had the stream or brook not babbled or trickled."

To the Soil, Our Soul Returns

"We build empires in the sky, but it is the earth that will cradle us in the end—not as failure, but as homecoming. For dust is not our ruin, but our root."

Transformation of Weight to Embrace

"Within the dance of elements, a stone's steadfast weight transforms into the gentle embrace of a guardian, shielding a fragile leaf from the tempestuous winds of existence."

Unbroken Spirit

"The withering wind may bend the trees, but it cannot break their spirit."

Understanding Nature's Language

"Every living thing in the universe can understand nature's language."

Universal Harmony of Music

"Music is all around you; all you have to do is listen to it."

Unveiling the Miraculous

"The profound harmony between the seen and the unseen is revealed by miracles, hidden within the mysteries of nature, demonstrating that the extraordinary frequently arises from the ordinary."

Vibes and Tribes

"Your vibes attract your tribe. Choose to exude positivity, love, and good energy."

Whispers of Dreams Carried by the Wind

"The wind wanders where whispers of dreams and secrets lead, carrying tales of distant lands and forgotten stories."

Whispers of Nature's Cycles

"Nature whispers in cycles, a timeless ballet of birth, bloom, and the quiet embrace of dusk—an eloquent metaphor for the poetry of our own existence."

Wind's Dual Role

"While the wind may break the branches, it also scatters the seeds for new growth."

Wisdom from Life's Challenges

"Life's challenges can be the ominous clouds that gather, but remember, they precede the refreshing rain of wisdom and renewal."

Woods of Discovery

"The woods are a place where one can both lose themselves and find themselves."

Yearning for the Wind

"When the wind leaves, kites lose their muse, dry leaves find their resting place, and trees stand in stillness, yearning for its return."

Whispers of the Divine

Cosmic connection

"Our connections transcend space and time, tying us to the eternal dance of the universe, from the depths of our souls to the farthest reaches of the cosmos."

- Shree Shambav

Aum's Cosmic Aim

"Aum is the bow, and the soul is its arrow, aiming steadfastly at the target of cosmic bliss, releasing the profound potential within to hit the mark of transcendence."

Awakening Earth

"As the Earth awakens in a riot of mud-luscious beauty, we are reminded of nature's strength and resiliency."

Awakening Through Meditation

"Within the depths of meditation, our inner selves awaken, nurturing the growth of our higher faculties, and in this transformation, we find the path to comprehend the ultimate truth."

Beneath Our Feet, A Prayer

"The Earth does not speak in thunder or boast in flame—it whispers through roots and rivers, in the quiet patience of stone, reminding us that real strength is still, slow, and sustaining."

Boundless and Eternal

"Grace is boundless and eternal, and it washes over us and carries us to new and better shores like the ocean."

Carrying Joy

"If you carry joy in your heart, the burdens of life will become lighter, and your journey will become a dance of joy and contentment."

Celestial Melody

"Music is a celestial gift of the Supreme, a melody that transcends time and touches the soul."

Celestial Pirouette

"Stars pirouette on the waves of time in the cosmic theatre, a poignant reminder that even the farthest luminaries can affect the ebb and flow of our emotions."

Celestial Threads

"In the cosmic ballet of existence, our connections are celestial threads, weaving the tapestry of our lives into the grand symphony of the universe, harmonising the dance of souls across the vast expanses of time."

Celestial Whispers

"Amidst the silent void, celestial music whispers secrets of the universe, resonating in the hearts of stargazers, revealing cosmic mysteries that transcend time and space."

Contemplating the Tapestry

"Contemplate the cosmic tapestry, understanding that the universe unfolds in harmonious unity - every element, every heartbeat, resonating in you, with you, and purposefully for you."

Core of Religions

"Religions, like the various forms of water in nature, may differ in their practices and beliefs, but at their core, they all strive to lead us to a deeper understanding of the fundamental truth that unites us."

Cosmic Connections

"Our cosmic connections are constellations of shared experiences, with each star representing a memory, lighting up the night sky of our lives."

Cosmic Reflections

"In the river of the cosmos, stars cast their reflections, creating a dance of wonder on the ripples of existence."

Cultivating Higher Faculties

"In the stillness of inner self-exploration, we cultivate our higher faculties, and only then can we hope to fathom the profound mysteries and ultimate truths that shape our existence."

Dancing with Life

"To be a saint or yogi is not to escape life, but to dance with it, to sing with it, and to let your heart be touched by the beauty and chaos of the world."

Dawn's Flight

"With the birth of a new day, let your heart take flight on the wings of appreciation, painting the sky of your life with the hues of love and thankfulness."

Depths of Grace

"The 'ocean of grace' is vast and infinite, with unfathomable depths and never-ending tides."

Discovering Nature's Beauty and Power

"In the wild, I discover the beauty and power of nature, and I am reminded of my place in the universe."

Diversity of Spiritual Paths

"Just as a drizzling droplet, a stagnant pond, a gushing river, and a tranquil stream are all manifestations of water, so various religions reflect the diverse ways humanity seeks to connect with the universal truth."

Divine Plan

"God has a reason for your misery. A reason for your toil and a reward for your devotion. Believe that He will bring the good people into your way of life at the correct time and for the right reasons."

Divine Symphony

"In the symphony of life, music is a divine gift from the Supreme, a harmonious thread that connects us all."

Dreams Whispered to the Stars

"He whispered his dreams to the stars, praying they would lead him to his destiny."

Drops in the Ocean of Grace

"We are but a few drops in the ocean of grace, carried by the currents to the shores of salvation."

Dwellers in the Consciousness of AUM

"Living in the consciousness of AUM is to dwell in the sacred temple of awareness, where the symphony of existence reverberates in every heartbeat, and the soul finds its eternal rhythm."

Earthly Stars

"Fireflies dance in the darkness, illuminating the world with their delicate radiance as if the stars have descended to Earth."

Earth's Symphony

"In the whispers of the wind and the murmur of the streams, the Earth composes odes of timeless beauty, inviting us to listen to its symphony."

Embracing Innocence

"Bring back your innocence and let the child who exists within realise the difference between right and wrong. Connect with beauty, not ugliness, and be cautious about what you infuse into your physical self and mind, as there is nothing more precious and worthy than the innocent child's heart."

Embracing Life's Divinity

"You do not become a saint or yogi by not living life; you become one by embracing every moment, every experience, and finding divinity in the ordinary."

Enchanting Fireflies

"Fireflies, like tiny beacons of light, enchant the night with their ethereal glow, reminding us of the beauty in simplicity."

Enriching Diversity of Religions

"Just as flowers add a unique charm to a garden, different religions enrich humanity with their profound wisdom and teachings."

Essence of Humanity

"Purusha, the essence of humanity, sometimes leans towards a chosen few, leaving the rest in the shadows of preference."

Essential Elements

"Grace is the water that keeps us alive, the wind that keeps us moving, and the light that illuminates our path."

Ethereal Symphony

"In the vast symphonic symphony of the cosmos, the stars and planets dance to the ethereal melody of celestial music, harmonising the universe with their celestial grace."

Facets of Water

"In the vast landscape of spirituality, religions are like the many facets of water - each distinct, yet all flowing towards the same ocean of truth and enlightenment."

Garden of Faith

"Like a garden adorned with a plethora of blossoms, the existence of various religions enhances our world, each offering a glimpse into the splendour of faith and belief."

Garden of Non-violence

"Master your mind, thoughts, and words in the garden of non-violence, where love and kindness are the nourishment for the soul's ascension."

Gift of Music

"The Supreme bestows upon us the precious gift of music, a language of emotions that speaks to the depths of our hearts."

Harbouring Illumination

"Inner stillness is not a destination; it's the quiet harbour from which the profound symphony of higher consciousness begins to play. It marks the genesis of a journey into the uncharted territories of inner activities, where the mind's silence orchestrates the magnificent functioning of a higher intelligence, casting the radiant glow of illumination upon the expanses of consciousness."

Healing Ocean

"The ocean of grace is a source of healing and renewal, a place of rest and restoration for the weary and broken-hearted."

Illuminating Flames

"When you go down in flames, let it be a blaze that illuminates your path forward, guiding you towards a new beginning."

Impartial Nature

"Prakriti, the essence of nature, remains impartial and holds no favourites in its embrace."

Imperishable Soul

"The soul is imperishable - unyielding against weapons, untouched by fire, undisturbed by water, and unwavering against the wind."

Integral Part of the Universe

"In the vast expanse of the universe, realise that you are not merely an observer but an integral part—everything exists in you, with you, and for you."

Interconnectedness in Nature

"In nature, everything is interconnected and woven together in a delicate dance of harmony and balance."

Journey Inward to See God

"The quest to see God is a journey inward, where the heart serves as the compass to the divine's omnipresence."

Journey of the Soul

"The soul is a traveller on a journey, released from the bounds of earthly existence and transported to the light of its true home."

Language of Music

"In the harmonious notes of music, the spirit speaks a language beyond words, unravelling the mysteries of life and ushering in a tranquil serenity that dissolves all conflict."

Language of the Spirit

"Music, the divine language of the spirit, holds the key to unlocking life's mysteries. It brings about deep peace, putting an end to the conflict and discord in our hearts and bringing our existence into harmony."

Liberation in the Wild

"When I walk into the wild, where nature's beauty and mystery unfold before me, my spirit is set free."

Life as a River

"Life is a river, flowing towards a 'Life in fullness,' and it marks the beginning of a new and improved life. It simply paves the way for a higher form of life."

Magical Night Sky

"The night sky transforms into a magical stage, where stars perform an eternal dance upon the fluid ripples of time."

Manifestation of Love

"AUM is the divine manifestation of Supreme Love, a river that flows to embrace both you and all creation. When you immerse yourself in AUM, you become one with the bliss of Supreme love, a boundless ocean of joy and connection."

Maya's Spell

"Maya, the illusion, often casts a powerful spell over the soul. Does this imply that Maya is mightier than the soul?"

Oasis of the Heart

"In the heart's desert, love and kindness are the life-giving waters, and mastery of mind, thought, and word is the bridge to a higher self, where the soul truly elevates."

Ocean of Grace

"Grace is a vast and deep ocean, but it is always present and available for those who seek it."

Pilgrimage of the Heart

"Spirituality is a quest for the extraordinary in the ordinary, for the sacred in the mundane. It's a pilgrimage of the heart where silence serves as the guide, and love is the destination."

Power of AUM

"AUM, the word of power and light, emerges not just from the depths of the mind, but also from higher planes of intuition, illuminating the path to transcendence."

Power of Prayer

"It only takes one prayer to change everything; God listens to your heart, even if you can't put your prayer into words."

Prakruti's Dance

"Prakruti plays no favourites; in the dance of survival, both the tiger and the deer must run. The tiger pursues its prey, and the deer sprints to escape its predator."

Ray of Hope

"Even in the dead of night, there is always a ray of hope waiting to lead us to a better tomorrow."

Realm of the Soul

"In the realm of the soul, weapons fail, fire quivers, water retreats, and the wind bows in reverence, for its essence is beyond the reach of destruction."

Resilience in Darkness

"Our resilience and courage shine through in our darkest moments, just as the night sky unveils its stars in the darkest hours."

Resonance of OM

"OM, the eternal melody of love, compassion, and bliss, resonates within the soul, harmonising the symphony of existence."

Sacred Tapestry

"Spirituality unfolds like a sacred tapestry in the stillness of the soul. Each thread of reflection and prayer crafts a deeper connection to the cosmos, reminding us that we touch the divine within our inner sanctum."

Sanctuary of Inner Peace

"In the heart's stillness, we find the sanctuary of inner peace, a place where life's storms may rage outside, but tranquillity reigns within."

Secrets to the Moon

"In the night's darkness, he whispered his secrets to the moon, believing that it would keep him safe."

Secrets to the Wind

"She whispered her secrets to the wind, hoping they would be carried away by the wind and never heard by anyone else."

Seeds of Transformation

"The seeds of transformation are found in the darkest moments, for it is in adversity that we find our true strength."

Seeking God Within

"To see God in every corner of the world, one must first learn to behold Him within the depths of the heart."

Sorrow Whispered to the Universe

"She whispered her sorrow to the universe, hoping it would understand."

Soul's Gaze

"The eyes alone cannot perceive the omnipresent, for God reveals Himself through the soul's gaze."

Soul's Inner Vision

"The soul's inner eye sees beyond the bounds of the material world, revealing an infinite universe of possibilities."

Spiritual Compass

"Amidst the chaos of existence, spirituality is the compass that points us inward, where we discover the boundless wellspring of peace, the infinite garden of wisdom, and the eternal sanctuary of the soul."

Spring's Vivacity

"Mud-luscious and puddle-wonderful, spring is the season that brings life and colour to the world."

Steps to Immortality

"Create the human race, become a human, and weave an inviolable work. Sharpen the shining spears you will use to cut the path to the immortal; those who are aware of the hidden planes create the steps by which the Gods attain immortality. You are seers of truth."

Stories of Perseverance

"From the smallest blade of grass to the vast expanse of the cosmos, everything in nature holds a story of perseverance, growth, and evolution."

Sunrise and Sunset

"Each sunrise and sunset, a stanza from Earth's eternal poem, etching verses of wonder and gratitude in our hearts."

Symphony of Existence

"OM springs forth from the profound realisation of the unity of the supreme and self, cosmos and light, man and nature, thing and thought, expression and freedom—a symphony of existence echoing through the essence of life itself."

Symphony of the Heavens

"The celestial music that graces the heavens is a symphony of celestial bodies, each note an ode to the eternal dance of creation and destruction, echoing throughout the expanse of the cosmos."

The Inner Eye of the Soul

"The inner eye of the soul allows us to see the splendour and wonder that exists in the world, illuminating the path to tranquillity and fulfilment."

Transcending to Higher Consciousness

"Each soul 'transcends to a realm of higher consciousness and expanded existence, experiencing liberation from the burdens of the physical world.'"

Twilight's Embrace

"In the embrace of twilight, fireflies emerge like tiny miracles, painting the night with their sparkling grace."

Unfold Your Myth

"Unfold your myth and allow it to lead you to your true purpose." You have a unique story within you that is just waiting to be discovered and shared with the world."

Unfolding Heart's Wings at Dawn

"Let your heart unfold its wings in the soft embrace of dawn, acknowledging the delicate miracles of love that lie ahead on the canvas of a new day."

Unity in Cosmic Dance

"Within the cosmic dance of existence, recognise the profound connection: all things, from the tiniest atoms to the grand galaxies, converge in you, with you, and ultimately, for you."

Unlocking Truths Through Meditation

"Meditation is the key to unlocking our higher faculties, allowing us to understand the profound truths that lie beyond the surface of existence."

Weaving Saints

"In the tapestry of existence, saints and yogis are those who weave the threads of everyday life with threads of profound awareness and love."

Whisper of Appreciation

"She whispered her appreciation to the world, expressing gratitude for all the blessings in her life."

Whispered Apologies

"He whispered his apologies to those he had wronged, hoping for forgiveness."

Whispered Desires

"He whispered his deepest desires to the universe, praying that they would manifest into reality."

Whispers to the Wind

"He whispered his fears to the wind, hoping that it would carry them away."

Wilderness Refuge

"The wilderness is my refuge, where I find solace, tranquillity, and a connection to something greater than myself."

Wisdom of Nature's Patterns

"Nature's wisdom speaks softly through its patterns, reminding us to live in synchronicity with the rhythms of life."

Worship with Love

"Worship with Love and Praise, Gratitude and Thanksgiving, Confession and Humility, these are the five concepts to offer to the Higher Power, which is called prayer… just uniting with the Absolute Truth. All done while passionately concentrating on the heart."

Shades of Existence

Light of Life

"We discover the profound beauty of our mortality, where each breath is a treasure and every heartbeat a testament to the journey, in the delicate balance between the light of life and the shadow of death."

- *Shree Shambav*

Alchemy of Oneness

"In the sacred alchemy of self-discovery, the key to oneness lies in the courageous release of imprisoning ideas and the emancipation from the clutches of lower emotions. To merge with your higher self is to embark on the sacred pilgrimage of character-building—a transformative process where authenticity unfurls its wings and soars above the confines of the mundane."

Appreciation through Acceptance

"Embracing the inevitability of death can lead individuals to a deeper appreciation of the world's beauty and the gifts of life."

Attaining Everlasting Life

"If one could learn to die while living, a voluntary death at will, one gains life everlasting, free from the endless cycle of births and deaths and rebirths."

Awakening to Truth

"This place is a fantasy or delusion. The only person who thinks it is true is asleep. Death then appears like the dawn, and you awaken laughing at what you had mistaken for grief."

Belief in Reality

"Believe in reality rather than mirrors."

Beyond Reflection

"No mirror can reflect you."

Born with Wings

"We were born with wings; why do we choose to crawl through life instead?"

Breaking the Cycle

"Destroy your desire to end the greed and destroy the greed to end the fear."

Continuation Beyond Death

"Death is not the end of a person's life. It's just the end of a significant individuality."

Continuation of Existence

"Nothing ever truly dies; it simply ceases to exist in one form before resuming it in another."

Control of Destiny

"Through your thoughts and actions, you are in control of your destiny and future."

Cycle of Birth and Death

"Birth follows death, just as waking follows sleep."

Death's Doorway

"The prison of life and the bondage of grief are the same. Darkness cannot engulf the light. And no death can bring life to an end."

Defiance in Life and Death

"I am not afraid of death, for while I am living, death shall not conquer me. And when I am gone, I shall not truly live."

Defiant Confrontation

"Fearless, I face the spectre of death. For as long as I breathe, death is but a distant visitor. And when my breath ceases, I shall no longer be bound by the limitations of mortal existence."

Dispelling Ignorance by the Master

"A true Master dispels the darkness of ignorance and leads the individual to ultimate truth."

Dispelling Maya

"The greatest of Maya (deceit; illusion) is not knowing one's true self. The illusion vanishes once this ignorance is removed."

Dispelling Uncertainty

"When people understand the basic truth, all uncertainty will disappear like darkness before the radiant light."

Dive Deep

"The essence of the soul is veiled to those who only scratch the surface of life; only those who dare to dive deep can discover the priceless treasure within."

Doorway to Fullness

"Death is the doorway to a 'Life in fullness,' and it marks the beginning of a new and better life. It merely paves the way for a higher form of life."

Droplet of Consciousness

"The human spirit is akin to a droplet of consciousness originating from the vast ocean of consciousness, taking the form of an individual spirit shrouded in different garbs. It is intriguing to note that despite our proximity to one another; we remain distant and disconnected."

Emancipation through Death

"Death is the ultimate emancipator of the soul, for it frees us from the physical cage that we call the body. Even death itself cannot bind the phoenix, which rises from the ashes to fly once more. If such a glorious creature can be unchained from the fetters of mortality, why should we, with our limited earthly existence, linger in this temporary abode? Let us instead long for the home that awaits us, where we may soar freely in the boundless expanse of eternity."

Embrace Karmic Obligation

"Embrace your karmic obligation, for the choices you make today sculpt the masterpiece of your future."

Embrace Simplicity

"Live this life like an empty vessel, devoid of worldly embellishments and distractions. Embrace simplicity, and let go of the need to adorn yourself on the outside, for it is the emptiness within that allows you to be truly filled."

Embrace of Spirituality

"Forsake the flesh for the spirit. Learn to die so that you may begin to live."

Empowerment through Karma

"Empower yourself by understanding the Law of Karma; it's the compass to navigate your destiny."

Essence of the Soul

"The essence of the soul is the purest form of energy that illuminates the path to self-realisation and leads to the realisation of the ultimate truth."

Eternal Architects

"The profound forces of love and death stand as the eternal architects of change. Love, the gentle sculptor, moulds moments into memories, and death, the cosmic conductor, orchestrates the poignant symphony of transformation that resonates throughout the tapestry of existence."

Eternal Cycle

"Nobody comes and nobody goes"

Eternal Dwelling Place

"Oh human, fear not the inevitability of death, for there is an eternal dwelling place, which is Brahman. This divine entity is none other than your very own Atman, residing in the inner sanctum of your heart. By cleansing your heart and contemplating upon this immaculate, imperishable, and unchanging Self, you will achieve immortality."

Eternal Nature

"Nothing perishes... nothing dies."

Eternal Nature of Life

"Life is the sea."

Eternal Progression of Life

"Life is eternal as time progresses from eternity to eternity, having on one form after another, appearing, disappearing, and reappearing like waves on the sea."

Eternal Soul

"How can death exist for the Eternal Soul, which exists beyond time, space, and causation?"

Existence of Brahman

"No one truly comes, and no one goes. The only thing that exists is Brahman - the ultimate reality."

Fear of Death

"Amidst the dance of existence, death stands as the profound fear shared by all living beings, an inevitable truth etched in the very fabric of life."

Flame in Darkness

"When life's storms rage, hold onto the flame in your heart because it will see you through the darkest nights."

Flame of Life

"Life is a pure flame, and we live by an invisible sun within us – 'Light of Life.'"

Flickering Candle

"Life is as flickering as a candle."

Focus on the Atman

"In the pursuit of spiritual enlightenment, it is essential for seekers to gradually and patiently detach themselves from all mental distractions, using the power of a resolute and astute will. Their minds should be firmly fixed on the Atman, with no room for any other thoughts or distractions. Even when the mind wanders restlessly, it must be redirected and subjugated to the Atman alone. This requires persistent effort, but the rewards of a focused and tranquil mind are immeasurable."

Gateway to a Fuller Life

"Death is only the gateway to a fuller life."

Grace in Life and Death

"If you have lived your life with grace, it becomes remarkably important that you die with grace."

Guru's Ever-Present Love

"Those who love and revere their Guru never feel alone in life."

Hope from Within

"A light of hope that shines from your heart illuminates your soul."

Illusion of Maya

"Birth and death are the two opposite ends of the illusory world of Maya, which is unreal."

Illusory Nature of the World

"The world is an illusion. We must take it seriously because it is the closest thing to reality that we can comprehend."

Immortality of the Soul

"You cannot die because you were never born."

Inner Purification

"Like a blacksmith forges steel in the fire, inner purification tempers your character, making you resilient and unbreakable in the face of life's challenges."

Interconnectedness of Souls

"The inner eye of the soul sees the interconnectedness of all things and serves as a constant reminder of our place in the grand scheme of things."

Journey of the Soul

"The journey of the soul is one of transformation, with each experience shaping and moulding its essence, leading to a more expansive and enlightened existence."

Joy in the Journey

"Life is a journey; what matters is not where we end up, but how we got there. Concentrate on the journey rather than the destination. We find joy in doing rather than in accomplishing."

Karma's Guidance

"Embrace the Law of Karma as your guiding light, illuminating the path to a brighter future."

Karmic Destiny

"Paint your future with the brushstrokes of conscious actions, like an accomplished artist, for you hold the palette of your karmic destiny."

Law of Reproduction

"Because like begets like, a paddy seed cannot create wheat. Every living being developed from a seed according to a preset pattern of life determined by the seed's inherent nature."

Life as a Flowing River

"Life is a river, flowing ceaselessly through the unreal world until it merges with the eternal sea of existence."

Life as an Unending River

"Life is an unending river that flows through the transient world until it merges with the boundless ocean of existence. Therefore, death signifies not the end of life, but the culmination of individual identity."

Limits of Comprehension

"Many things are beyond our comprehension; we can only perceive them; we cannot explain them with our intelligence."

Loneliness vs. Solitude

"Loneliness is the feeling of having no one there for you, while solitude is a choice to be alone with one's thoughts."

Longing for the Supreme

"When you long for the Supreme as much as you long for your last breath in your dire situation, we will see the light at the end of the tunnel."

Love and Death

"In the grand theatre of life, only love and death hold the power to transform all things, for they are the silent architects of our deepest joys and our darkest sorrows."

Love and Death as Constants

"The two constants that shape the very essence of existence are love, the force that ignites our souls, and death, the harbinger of our final journey, crafting a story only they can narrate."

Love and Death as Weavers

"Through the tapestry of time, love and death stand as the master weavers, altering the threads of our destinies with a tenderness that mends and a cruelty that rends, leaving no heart untouched by their transformative touch."

Material Possessions

"We came into this world with nothing and one day we will depart from it with nothing."

Maya's Enigma

"We live in Maya's world, which is an enigmatic puzzle shrouded in mystery. Nobody can control anyone else or the events that occur around us. Life moves so quickly. One moment you're on top of the world, and the next…"

Maya's Illusion of Birth and Death

"Birth and death are two of Maya's juggling acts, and in this illusion, the process of creation and cessation merely serve as doors of entry and exit on the stage of Maya."

Merging with the Supreme Soul

"The sun's reflection merges with the sun itself as the water in the pond absorbs it. Similarly, when the thoughts are annihilated through meditation, the individual soul merges itself into the Supreme soul. It is the goal of life, and one can experience it right here, right now, while still alive."

Nature's Canvas

"Nature is an infinitely beautiful canvas, and every stroke of colour is a brush of bliss."

New Existence

"Death is not an end, but a doorway to a life in fullness. It marks the beginning of a new and better existence, paving the way for a higher form of life."

Path to Peace

"Destroy your desire to end the greed, destroy the greed to end the fear. Once fear is gone, you rest in peace."

Perceived World

"The world we perceive, with its plethora of names, forms, and attributes constrained by time, space, and causation."

Perception of the Divine

"The illumined one perceives the Divine in all beings, in all directions, and at all times, as a universal life force surging within every soul."

Perpetual Nature of Death

"Recognise that death is not an arbitrary event that takes place after we die. It occurs at all times in our lives!"

Post-Life Path

"The path we take after death is determined by what we did while we were living."

Power of Prayer

"Prayer is to the soul what wings are to a bird. In the heart's silence, God speaks. Even when mingled with cries and commotion, it reaches God's ears."

Power of the Mind

"The mind is the source of creation; wherever the mind exists, so does the world."

Purpose of Existence

"Isn't it unfortunate that we live without a reason or purpose for our existence on this planet?"

Reality of Corporeality

"Nothing corporeal is real; only the incorporeal is devoid of deception."

Realm of Thoughts

"All souls live in close communion with one another in the world of thoughts, where thought vibrations are the only means of communication between souls."

Reciprocal Nourishment

"Death nourishes life and life brings light to death."

Religious Diversity

"In the vast garden of humanity, diverse religions bloom like exquisite flowers, teaching us to appreciate the various paths that lead to a higher truth."

Resilient Heart

"When the world seems dark and uncertain, cling to the unwavering resilience of your heart."

Return Home

"Why should one weep on their departure? Are they not returning home? It is within our power to consciously work towards re-linking the strand of life in us and attain that end."

Rising Above

"The boundless joy can be yours, only if we know how to rise above the physical vesture, break the veil of boundary and catch the sublime vision which comes to the pure."

Science of the Soul

"The science of the soul invites us to discover the true nature of who we are beyond our physical form, and to awaken to the interconnectedness of all things."

Secret of Death

"Our quality of life will be different if we discover the secret of death! Our perspective on life, our comprehension of death, and our attitude towards it will all change."

Seed of the Word

"The seed of the Word sown by the sower (the Master) ever resides within the depths of his disciple's soul, and with time, it will sprout, blossom, and bear fruit."

Seer and Seen

"The existence of worlds depends on the presence of the seer and the seen. The seer, who handles all things of sight, is necessary for the existence of the seen."

Seize Control of Karma

"Unlock the secrets of your future and seize control of your karma's course."

Simplicity of Being

"Live this life simply, as empty as possible, live this life like an empty pot, not like decoration outside it."

Simplicity of Life

"There is no purpose in life; life is a purpose; life is simple; just appreciate who you are, how you look and be delightful."

Solace in Death's Realm

"While I am alive, death dances on the periphery, unable to ensnare me. And in the realm of the dead, I find solace, for there I am free from the shackles of life."

Soul's Transformation

"The journey of the soul is one of transformation, with each experience shaping and moulding its essence, leading to a more expansive and enlightened existence."

Steadfast Heart

"Don't let your heart falter in the face of life's challenges; let it be the steady beat that propels you forward."

Stillness of the Mind in Yoga

"The stillness of the mind attained through the practice of yoga leads to the realisation of the Atman by the aspirant."

Tranquil Silence

"When I am silent, I enter a realm where everything is harmonious, tranquil, colourful, and beautiful."

Transcendence of Limitations

"To truly understand the boundless potential of our minds and souls, we must transcend our physical limitations and develop the ability to perceive without sight, listen without hearing, hold on without touch, and move without motion."

Transcendence of Music

"Music has the power to transport a person from the earthly material plane, elevate one's emotions, and aid in the flow of hidden tears without the individual's awarness."

Transcending Materialism

"While we are content with what we see, feel, and touch, we have been driven away from the materialistic way of looking at things because we lack knowledge and experience of the noumenon."

Transcending the Flesh

"It is in the flesh and through flesh that we come to Him who is beyond the flesh."

Transience of Life

"Every person who enters this world will depart from it someday, which is a poignant truth."

Transience of Youth

"Youth is as transient as a flower."

Transient Existence

"What did not exist in the beginning and will not exist in the future or now?"

Treasures of Spirituality

"Life offers a chance to gather the treasures of spirituality that remain concealed within us, often overlooked and unknown."

Understanding Maya's Deception

"Maya (illusion) denotes profound ignorance. Ignorance causes worldly pain. In this world, there can be no pain or suffering. If such a thing as pain and suffering existed."

Unified Soul

"When you realise you are nothing more than a part of a superior soul, you stop discriminating and disliking one another, you lose your greed and desire, and you lose all worth in this materialistic world."

Unknown Realm

"We don't know what death will be like?"

Veil of Death

"None who have died return to tell their tale, for those who recount the story have themselves succumbed to the veil of death."

Vivid Destiny

"In the fabric of existence, your past deeds painted the background, but it is your present deeds that add vivid colours to the canvas of your destiny."

SHREE SHAMBAV

Blossoming Life

A Priceless Dance

In the tranquil hush, a flower takes its stance,

By the pond, 'neath the tree, in nature's sweet romance,

Across the plains and down the verdant lanes,

On ridges high and where the wild edge remains.

They sparkle like stars in the evening's embrace,

Waving, twirling, in nature's tender grace,

With flies and butterflies, the secrets they share,

As if they've known each other beyond time, beyond care.

In their delicate petals, strength does reside,

Soft, yet resilient, against the wind's stride,

Fleeting moments, yet so self-assured,

In the language of blossoms, their truth is assured.

Approach the flower with stillness and grace,

Open your heart and your ears to embrace,

The euphoria of blooms in their silent song,

In the gentle breeze, love's whispers prolong.

A whisper of love in fragrant diffusion,

Spreading joy, sparking nature's fusion,

Such beauty they bring it's a magical sight,

For they make the world shine, bathed in their light.

Have you met these blooms in your lifetime's quest?

Though they know not of worry nor rest,

In their belief, they shall forever remain,

Infinite moments in life's fleeting domain.

Your life, too, is a priceless bloom,

LIFE CHANGING JOURNEY

Not meant for despair, nor darkened gloom,

You're not a burden upon this earthly plane,

Dance like a flower, both fierce and humane.

Embrace your existence in moments divine,

Leave memories behind, like stars that brightly shine,

In the grand tapestry of life, play your part,

For you are a masterpiece, a work of living art.

- Shree Shambav

Life Coach and Philanthropist

Shree Shambav is the visionary founder of the Shree Shambav Ayur Rakshita Foundation (www.shambav-ayurrakshita.org). He founded this institution with a lofty goal: to recognise human identity across gender, ethnicity, and nationality. Through this organisation, he wants to assist all communities in realising their full potential and the intrinsic beauty of life.

Shree Shambav, a Life Coach, is dedicated to supporting people on their journeys of self-discovery and empowerment. He assists people in discovering who they are, determining what inspires and drives them, and overcoming limiting ideas. His approach clarifies what one wants in life, assisting people through goal-setting and a step-by-step process for achieving them. He empowers people to make deliberate and responsible decisions, allowing them to identify their blind spots and evolve as individuals via the use of numerous strategies and tools.

The foundation's bold, uncompromising, and compassionate ventures are always aimed at initiating the "Inner Transformation" process. They focus on spiritual growth, personal growth, and self-healing while emphasising that true progress lies in "Inclusive Growth and Co-existence." This philosophy drives all their initiatives, encouraging a holistic approach to development and well-being.

Under Shree Shambav's leadership, the foundation has launched several impactful movements:

Shree Shambav Green Movement: This mission is to create a healthy, green, and clean earth through responsible water conservation and greening initiatives. The movement strives to make the world a green paradise by encouraging sustainable living and environmental responsibility.

Shree Shambav Vidya Vedhika (Vizhuthugal): This project aims to help students and children by offering training, books, stationery, and uniforms. It aims to provide the next generation with the tools and resources they need to excel both academically and personally.

Shree Shambav and his foundation exemplify the spirit of compassion, transformation, and inclusive growth via their work, which has a profound impact on individuals and communities around the world. His work exemplifies the power of acknowledging and nourishing the human spirit, creating a world in which everyone can reach their full potential and appreciate the beauty of life.

TESTIMONIALS

Journey of Soul - Karma - "We die in our twenties and are buried at eighty." Remember that nothing can stop someone who refuses to be stopped. "Most people do not fail; they simply give up." Shree Shambav deserves full credit. It allowed me to sit and consider what I might miss out on in life. The author has delved into every aspect of our daily lives. How can a seemingly insignificant change in these seemingly insignificant details bring us such joy? The Soul of Journey teaches you the "art of living" as well as the "art of dying."

Twenty + One Series - The rich cultural heritage offered a host of twenty + one short stories with incredible imagination, morals and values prevalent at a given time, influencing how people respond to a crisis or any situation. The author has recreated images with universal values and morals. The plentiful of fascinating from faraway lands would leave the modern play and story writers a cringe. The book supports trust and immeasurable values, instilling hope for the new generations.

Death - "Shree Shambav's 'Death - Light of Life and the Shadow of Death' is an extraordinary masterpiece that delves deep into the profound questions surrounding our existence and mortality. The book's opening statement, 'Nothing ever truly dies; it simply ceases to exist in one form before resuming it in another,' sets the stage for a thought-provoking exploration of death's multifaceted nature. Shambav's remarkable ability to navigate the philosophical complexities of death and our universal fear of it is both enlightening and comforting. This book is a testament to the power of understanding and acceptance."

Whispers of Eternity - "Reading 'Whispers of Eternity' by Shree Shambav was a transformative experience that left me captivated from beginning to end. Each section of this exquisite collection delves into the myriad facets of existence, offering poignant reflections on life, death, and everything in between. Shree Shambav's verses are a testament to the beauty of language and the power of expression, inviting readers to embark on a journey of self-discovery and spiritual awakening. Whether celebrating life's simple joys or grappling with the complexities of human emotion, this book is a timeless companion that speaks to the heart and soul of every reader."

Life Changing Journey Series - "Life Changing Journey Series II Inspirational Quotes" is a remarkable collection that illuminates the path to self-discovery and personal growth. With its inspiring quotes and insightful reflections, this book serves as a beacon of light in a world often shrouded in darkness. Each quote offers wisdom, guidance, and encouragement, reminding readers of their inner strength and resilience. A must-read for anyone seeking inspiration and enlightenment.

Learn To Love Yourself – "A Heartfelt Guide to Authentic Self-Love." "Learn to Love Yourself" invites readers on a transformative journey to embrace their true essence in a world often focused on external validation. Through ten insightful chapters, it gently reveals principles of genuine self-love, guiding readers to deepen their connection with themselves. Beyond surface positivity, it encourages the cultivation of resilient self-acceptance, from embracing one's unique qualities to setting empowering boundaries. With inspiring stories and practical wisdom, this book is a trusted companion on the path to inner peace, fulfilment, and joy, helping readers build lives that reflect their authentic selves.

The Power of Letting Go – This book has been a gift to my spiritual journey. Shree Shambav's insights into attachment, personal growth cycles, and forgiveness are enlightening. The concept of seven-year cycles resonated with me, helping me understand the natural phases of life. I feel more empowered to let go of what no longer serves me and step into a life of freedom and fulfilment. A truly beautiful read!

A Journey of Lasting Peace – "A Journey of Lasting Peace" feels like a trusted friend guiding you through the maze of self-discovery. The 18 transformative principles are both practical and deeply resonant, addressing everything from gratitude practices to the art of letting go. Each chapter is infused with warmth and wisdom, making it easy to apply the concepts to my life. I particularly appreciated the emphasis on physical health's connection to mental well-being; it served as a wake-up call for me to prioritise my health. This book is an invaluable resource for anyone serious about personal growth!

Astrology Unveiled Series – "Profound, Logical, and Inspiring". What stands out in Astrology Unveiled is the author's dedication to making Vedic astrology logical and approachable. Each concept flows naturally into the next, backed by examples and exercises. The insights into karma and life cycles add a philosophical depth rarely seen in astrology books. Perfect for anyone seeking spiritual growth alongside astrological knowledge!

The Entitlement Trap - "Thought-Provoking and Challenging" The book challenges readers to confront their own sense of entitlement, and that's not easy—but it's essential. The Entitlement Trap doesn't offer a one-size-fits-all approach. Instead, it's a thoughtful, layered examination of how entitlement can limit our growth. The chapter on "Defining Your Own Hill" was particularly impactful, as it pushed me to reconsider which challenges are truly worth pursuing. A thought-provoking read for those willing to do the inner work to create a life they can be proud of.

Whispers of a Dying Soul – "A Soul-Stirring Reflection on Life's Unspoken Truths" - *Whispers of a Dying Soul: Unspoken Regrets and Unlived Dreams"* is a deeply moving exploration of the unexpressed emotions and unfulfilled aspirations that shape our lives in ways we often don't realise. This book invites readers to confront the powerful, often hidden impact of regret while guiding them through a journey of introspection and healing. Each page opens a space to reflect on the choices that define us—from moments of unspoken love to neglected passions—offering a gentle reminder to live authentically and courageously.

Whispers of the Soul: A Journey Through Haiku - is a mesmerising collection that speaks directly to the heart. Each haiku is a delicate brushstroke capturing life's fleeting beauty and timeless wisdom, inviting readers into moments of deep reflection and peace. This book is a balm for the soul, guiding us to find meaning in stillness and connection in simplicity. The themes of nature, love, and mindfulness echo universal truths, resonating with quiet, powerful grace. It's a book to be savoured slowly, cherished deeply, and returned to often. Truly, it is a gift for anyone seeking calm and clarity in life's chaos.

Whispers of Silence - Unlocking Inner Power through Stillness by Shree Shambav is a rare gem that beckons readers to pause, reflect, and reconnect with their inner selves. In a world that never stops talking, this book offers a profound exploration of silence—not as a void but as a rich and transformative space.

From the first page, Shree Shambav's writing resonates deeply, blending scientific insights with spiritual wisdom in a way that feels both universal and deeply personal. The author's ability to bridge the tangible and the transcendent makes this book an invaluable guide for anyone navigating the chaos of modern life.

The Power of Words: Transforming Speech, Transforming Lives - The Power of Words is a profound and enlightening guide that has transformed the way I approach communication. Shree Shambav masterfully uncovers the hidden influence of our words on relationships, self-perception, and overall well-being. This book doesn't just teach you how to speak; it inspires mindful communication that fosters connection and trust. The insights on replacing negative patterns like gossip and judgment with kindness and authenticity are truly life-changing. The practical strategies and engaging narratives make it an invaluable resource for personal and professional growth. A must-read for anyone striving to communicate with intention, clarity, and compassion. Highly recommended!

The Art of Intentional Living: Minimalism for a Life of Purpose - "The Art of Intentional Living is a refreshing guide to finding clarity in a cluttered world. With practical wisdom and profound insights, it inspires you to simplify, prioritise, and live with purpose. A must-read for anyone seeking balance and fulfilment."

Awakening the Infinite: The Power of Consciousness in Transforming Life - "Awakening the Infinite is a transformative guide that expands the mind and nourishes the soul. With profound insights and practical wisdom, this book beautifully explores the power of consciousness, helping readers connect with their true purpose and inner potential. It is a journey of self-discovery, healing, and spiritual awakening, offering clarity and inspiration at every turn. A must-read for anyone looking to live with greater awareness, meaning, and authenticity."

Beyond the Veil: A Journey Through Life After Death:

"This book touched me in ways few others have—it's not just about death, but about life, meaning, and the vast unknown that connects them. Beyond the Veil offers a graceful blend of science and spirit, inviting us to explore the mystery with awe rather than fear. The stories, insights, and reflections linger in your heart long after the final page. A truly transformative read that brings light to the shadows of mortality. It reminded me that in embracing death, we truly learn how to live."

Bonds Beyond Blood:

"A profoundly moving story that reminds us family is not defined by blood, but by love, sacrifice, and the courage to heal. Every chapter touched my soul with its emotional truth and timeless wisdom. Through joy, grief, and redemption, this book captures the raw beauty of human connection. I saw reflections of my own family in its pages—both the pain and the hope. A powerful, unforgettable read that lingers long after the final word."

A Journey into Spiritual Maturity: 12 Golden Rules for Inner Transformation

"This book is a gentle yet powerful guide that awakened a deeper sense of purpose within me. Each golden rule felt like a mirror reflecting truths I needed to embrace. Shree Shambav's wisdom is timeless, poetic, and profoundly grounding. It's not just a read—it's a journey into the heart of who you truly are. A must-read for anyone seeking lasting peace, clarity, and inner transformation."

The Inner Battlefield: Overcoming the Enemies of the Mind and Soul:

"This book is a powerful revelation—an honest mirror to the battles we fight within. Every chapter is a step closer to clarity, peace, and emotional mastery. Shree Shambav brilliantly transforms ancient wisdom into practical guidance for modern souls. It awakened in me a new strength to face my fears and rise above inner turmoil. A must-read for anyone seeking true inner victory and lasting transformation."

The Seeker's Gold – Unlocking Life's Greatest Treasure

The Seeker's Gold is a soul-stirring masterpiece that goes far beyond the pursuit of wealth—it is a journey into the heart of what truly matters. Each chapter unfolds with poetic wisdom and emotional depth, revealing that life's real treasure is not found in riches but in the transformation of the self. As the protagonist evolves through trials, love, and profound realizations, so does the reader. This book is a mirror for every dreamer, a lantern for every seeker, and a companion for anyone walking the path of purpose. A timeless tale that stays with you long after the final page.

ACKNOWLEDGEMENTS

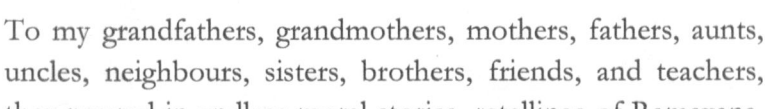

To my grandfathers, grandmothers, mothers, fathers, aunts, uncles, neighbours, sisters, brothers, friends, and teachers, they poured in endless moral stories, retellings of Ramayana, Mahabharata, Puranas, Upanishads, and so on.

My teachers, neighbours, and kindred souls. Who provided us with a stage to perform wonderful Puranic stories and were gracious enough to acknowledge our efforts.

The artists and translators of epics have served as a source of inspiration, invigorating our spirits, making these works accessible, and enabling us to grasp the profound depths and deeper dimensions they contain.

I also cherish the stimulating conversations I had with my wonderful mothers, Punitha Muniswamy and Uma Devi.

Our family's youngest member, Aadhya, who always overwhelmed me with questions, inspired this book.

I would likewise prefer to express gratitude to Mr Sivakumar, Mrs Roopa Sivakumar, Mr Akshaya Rajesh, Ms Akshatha Rajesh, Ms Apeksha Prabhu, Mr Akanksh Prabhu, Mr Nikash Sarasambi, Mrs Spoorthi Nikash for their valuable inputs.

I must thank Mr Rajesh, Mr Savan Prabhu, Mrs Revathi Rajesh, Mrs Rajani Sarasambi, and Mrs Manju Reshma, who encouraged me and often suggested writing a book. Their unwavering belief that I had something valuable to offer kept me going during my writing sessions.

Love you all,

Shree Shambav

www.shambav.org

shreeshambav@gmail.com

www.ingramcontent.com/pod-product-compliance
Lightning Source LLC
LaVergne TN
LVHW091540070526
838199LV00002B/143